TAKING STOCK

Taking Stock

A First Study of the Poetry of U.A. Fanthorpe

by Eddie Wainwright

PETERLOO POETS

First published in 1995
by Peterloo Poets
2 Kelly Gardens, Calstock, Cornwall PL18 9SA, U.K.

**A catalogue record for this book is available
from the British Library**

ISBN 1-871471-47-8

Printed in Great Britain by
Penwell Limited, Callington, Cornwall.

ACKNOWLEDGEMENTS:

This volume is published in association with Westminster College, Oxford.

To Diana, who gently
encouraged, reassured,
and sustained.

Contents

Page

Preface

This short study documents my personal exploration to date — there is much exploration still to be done — of five volumes of poetry, in a progressively detailed way, and I hope that readers embarking on a systematic study of the poetry will be eased into its depths rather than thrown in at the deep end. Before and during the writing of it, I made no study of any reviews and articles which U.A. Fanthorpe's work has stimulated; not out of arrogance, or a desire to re-invent the wheel every five minutes, or even to feel virtuous for going it alone, but because I wanted to project a unified, uncluttered view. So if emphases are misplaced, unimportant aspects highlighted or important ones glossed over, be it entirely on my head. (I have, in fact, included in an appendix some extracts from such reviews and articles as I read subsequent to completing the book which readers might find helpful to consult: which doesn't mean I don't reserve judgement on some of them.) For convenience, I have referred to the five individual volumes as follows: SE = *Side Effects*; ST = *Standing To*; VO = *Voices Off*; WB = *A Watching Brief*; N-V = *Neck-Verse*. The King Penguin *Selected Poems* of 1986 is sometimes referred to as 'Peng'.

Though it was the fact that the last-named has been designated an 'A' Level set text (by, to date, two Boards, Cambridge and N.E.A.B.) that triggered off the possibility of this study, it ranges over the entire five volumes, both to place *Selected Poems* in a wider and updated perspective, and also to try to demonstrate the unity and integrity of the poetry as a whole. I hope the study will be useful in both general and particular ways, though it is emphatically not a penny-in-the-slot kind of primer; on the other hand, I have not been unmindful of the kind of uses to which it may be put. At the risk of being at the outset tedious, I should like to explain myself more fully over this matter. Ch. One, inasmuch as the categories can be treated separately, is largely concerned with themes and "concerns", and Ch. Two with exegesis and illustrative close reading/analysis (as much of this as I had space to accommodate, for it is one of this poet's notable strengths to write in rich and subtle textures which need a matchingly sensitive and alert readership. Whether mine is so or not, I have at least tried to point the way). The views expressed, whether about particular poems' concerns or about points of detail — expressed as clearly and unequivocally as I could manage and without what I have good reason to call "reviewer's evasion" — are just mine and have no special authority beyond that of a committed and enthusiastic reader; and although the source of publication is the same as that of the poetry itself, what I say is not to be regarded as in the least definitive or exhaustive: the book, as the sub-title states, is "a first study". The interpretation and evaluation of poetry had better not be carved on stone tablets; meaning and significance — we are nowadays aware of this as perhaps never before — are the outcome of what is sometimes a long and complex negotiation between text and reader; and given even a high degree of reader competence (which this invariably approachable, more often than meets the eye complex or elusive poetry requires), there is sometimes arguably *some* room for manoeuvre such that one "reading" does not necessarily rule out of countenance another, even for the same reader at different times or states of responsiveness. I know all this is egg-suckingly obvious for some sophisticated and experienced readers; but we can all be caught napping. In brief, I have tried throughout to stay as attentive as the poetry expects me to be; but I in turn expect *my* readers to be aware that even my most persistent attempts to tease out the significance of themes and details is bound to be crude relative to what the poetry is doing, and may even perhaps sometimes be prolix and tedious. That this will be the fault of this writer and not of the poetry I shall say just this once. I hope readers, whether students or mere poetry lovers, will find their task of reading this book as profitable and rewarding to read as I did to write.

E.W.

Chapter One. Introduction: Mapping the Territory

' ... to chuse incidents and situations from common life, and ... to throw over them a certain colouring of the imagination, whereby ordinary things should be presented to the mind in an unusual way ... '
— Wordsworth: Preface to *Lyrical Ballads*, 1802

' ... turned up, now, the alley by the church,
That leads no whither ...
He glanced o'er books on stalls with half an eye ...
He took such cognisance of men and things,
If any beat a horse, you felt he saw;
If any cursed a woman, he took note;
Yet stared at nobody ... '
— Browning: "How it Strikes a Contemporary"

I shall try to find my bearings, and I hope to help readers to find theirs, by making a rather dense composite statement, as it were *horizontally*, along the volumes, about the poetry of U.A. Fanthorpe which it will be the task of the rest of this Cook's Tour of an Introduction to open out into a map of the territory of this study by taking some of its key words, phrases, and concepts, and relating them to the poetry generally, with profuse illustration. The second chapter will then take what seems the logical course of a *vertical*, book by book, chronological account, with some detailed consideration of important poems; four appendices will offer a biographical sketch, an interview and articles which readers may find helpful.

Already, in the mere 14 years of publication in volume form, inasmuch as cold statistics will help us to get our bearings, there have appeared some 210 poems in 324 pages, 70 of them reprinted in the *King Penguin* of 1986: already a considerable body of work. In fact, and though the focus of interest has in some ways and from time to time shifted from volume to volume, there has hitherto been a considerable consistency of preoccupation: stage centre are *people*. Apart from the pure "dramatic monologues" (a term I shall define in the next phase of the chapter), about 40 or so, there are in the five volumes about 100 studies of individuals or small groups (such as hospital staff or men on allotments). It is surely significant that nearly three quarters of UAF's output to date should be concerned so centrally with people: largely ordinary or unremarkable people (or people who to the casual glance would be unremarkable, which is a different matter); often failures, the dispossessed and seemingly inarticulate. But as we have them in the poetry, are they *really* "ordinary"? The way in which they are presented is sometimes a challenge to our preconceptions and misconceptions, as perhaps they were sometimes a challenge to the poet's. See, in this connection, "Patience Strong" in SE, in which the speaker — as I shall call her in first person singular poems that are not dramatic monologues — having categorically dismissed the work of

Patience Strong, has to regard a no-hoper (my term) fan of hers with some sympathy. Sometimes we are confronted with bullies, incompetents, and mis-managers, those who reduce people to meaningless and ignorable statistics — the "hospital" poems, as I shall call them, are a persistent group in which this happens. Increasingly, the range of subjects has included women (though UAF is not a politicised feminist of what the present writer has dubbed the Piranha School). Sometimes UAF's people speak for themselves, sometimes the poet is their alert presenter, sometimes sympathetic to some degree (precisely to *what* degree is a matter for the alert reader these poems expect), and sometimes critical. There is everywhere, or almost everywhere, an earnest attempt to be fair-minded, to record in an unpartisan and even-handed way; the degree of detachment exhibited is not, of course, indicative of not caring, but of a lack of sentimentality or facile involvement. Nor is this aspect of her writing incompatible with ironies (I use the plural at this point to suggest a spectrum of attitudes, from "dead pan" at one end to some fairly strong satire at the other: but there is no Pope-type invective). If the world of poetry since the Romantic movement has been largely concerned with willingly joining Romanticism or trying to beat it, between being post-Romantically Romantic (like, say, Tennyson) on the one hand, or trying to keep a balance, a restraint, which is to be a Classicist in some definitions of the term, and inasmuch as the crude old labels are helpful, then the poetry of Ursula Fanthorpe in some important respects leans in the direction of the "classical".

Detached, balanced, restrained, close observation seems to be what *my* observations have so far suggested: but what about the wit, the fun, the puns, the Alan Bennett-like demotic, the playful (and sometimes not so playful) conceits, the liveliness and curiosity and gusto? (UAF mentions in the Interview that Marvell is important to her: and yes, of course, the most urbane, civilised and perhaps intelligent member of the Metaphysical tribe must obviously be a congenial spirit. In fact, I suspect the entire School of Donne to be kindred spirits in some respects.) But if the language of the poems can be demotic, slangy or even downright crude where it has to be, the overall impression you have from reading even a small quantity of the poetry is of the sheer precision of so much of it, evidence of a great capacity for taking pains to "get it right". There is implicitly, and sometimes explicitly, an awareness of the power and potential of language: not for its own sake, not simply to make patterns or noises, but to communicate, to say things. There is a concomitant absence of an awareness of the limitations of language: many of our contemporaries are perhaps *too* aware of these, and are hobbled by them. Perhaps this is a way of saying that the poetry manoeuvres in areas where such limitations are no obstacle to communication (there is, for instance, no "metaphysics" in the strictly philosophical sense, and no attempt to plumb the depths of political or personal depravity with which we are currently perhaps too obsessed).

A similar precision is to be found in those poems which derive from a sense of the historical past — classical, pre- and post-Conquest, mediaeval and Renaissance: such poems are rooted in a *real*, not chocolate-boxy, world, or a merely picturesque rusticity, and UAF is too clear-eyed and honest to see things otherwise. One of her reviewers described her poetry as 'learned': I know what this critic meant, but the word is far too heavy-handed. I should prefer to say that these poems exhibit a wide and exact knowledge in the areas in which the poetry operates, in order to serve the needs of such poems. For instance, apart from wide and precise historical awareness and knowledge, there is a wide knowledge of plant life — flowers, trees, shrubs — their appearance, habitat, seasonal preferences, and so on: though she cannot be called a "Nature" poet except by stretching the term to breaking point. The word "history" has towed in its wake her awareness of "tradition": her belief in the necessity for an awareness of the past, the need for roots (rather, the awareness of the undeniable *fact* of them), an awareness of the old. (In another but surely related connection, many of UAF's *people* are old, and speak out of their awareness of times past and time passing.)

What features of this poetry, as I look over this attempt to make its composite portrait, have I not so far mentioned? The notion of "bearing witness" is important, sometimes explicitly but everywhere implicitly: the notion of "I was there and I saw this and wished to record it". (The Interview is quite explicit on this matter.) There is also the pervasive attempt in the poetry to dig through the seeming or the superficial or apparent to a firmer bedrock of truth: poem after poem is implicitly concerned with "truth-telling". Increasingly, too, there is the underpinning of the whole complex and fraught business of living by love; though there are very few entire love poems as such: but the positive is, as I've said, increasingly pervasive and apparent. The Interview says 'In order to write, I have to concentrate. And concentration is a form of love'. If this is too gnomic to communicate fully what it, I think, characteristically half conceals, for 'love' read "total commitment". Also typically, many a poem only becomes obliquely, or reveals itself truly as, a love poem towards its conclusion; and makes its full impact only in the light of this necessary ultimate dimension.

What all this surely amounts to is that this poetry communicates a positive sense of life being worth living, an affirmation of the value of the existence of a human society which, in spite of its complexities and its suffering, is endlessly worthwhile: this is no facile, head-in-sand (or in-air) affirmation. Perhaps we are already on the way to discovering what, in spite of the Interview disclaimer, is the appeal of U.A. Fanthorpe's poetry.

Some key concepts and phrases from this statement must now be explored in further detail. In view of the central interest in people which this poetry manifests and in view of her prolific use of the genre, it seems appropriate to begin with the dramatic monologue.

THE DRAMATIC MONOLOGUE

' ... a kind of drama specially suited to those whose main interest is in character', according to Alan Sinfield*. Briefly, a dramatic monologue is a speech, presented as a self-contained poem, in which the speaker, the "I", is not the poet; as compared, for instance, with the lyrics of Keats and Shelley, in which the "I" clearly and demonstrably *is* the poet. The genre is primarily a strategy for revealing characters in situations; it is as old as the Greeks, but its heyday was in the Victorian period. Its finest and most persistent exponent was Browning, whose importance to her UAF has confirmed in the Interview. In our own century its last famous exponents were Eliot, Pound, and Yeats, fifty and more years ago. UAF is one of the most notable of our contemporaries to use the form to any great extent. The writer of dramatic monologues is compelled to try to get inside the personality and experiences of somebody else; it is therefore an enforced mechanism for escaping from the arguably narrow confines of the limited self: you have to imagine a sympathetic projection of how it really feels to be somebody else, even somebody inimical to you, as are many of Browning's characters. Most of UAF's tend to be more sympathetic than otherwise. What such a poem presents is a character plus, implicitly, the poet's attitude to the character either in the selection of detail and/or the slant of the words (if that's different from "detail". It's really just another aspect): for if the speaker is not the poet, the poet's attitude to the speaker *has* to be implicit, never explicit, for the very frame created by the convention of the poem precludes this. The variety of UAF's speakers in her dramatic monologues ranges from small children to Jesus Christ, but there are also birds and beasts and Halley's comet! We shall sample some individual monologues in Ch. Two; suffice it for now to say that the volume which contains more of them than any other is *Standing To*; in *Voices Off*, *A Watching Brief* and *Neck-Verse*, third-person portraits seem to have been preferred. The Penguin *Selected Poems* has about 16 pure dramatic monologues out of a total of about 70 poems. (I keep saying "about" because an exact count depends on whether you count a poem with e.g. three sections as one poem or three). But dramatic monologues continue to appear in more recent volumes, and they are invariably amongst the most attractive and entertaining of the poems. Newcomers to the poetry of UAF might start with "Dear Mr Lee" and "The Cleaner". And of course, there is the poem on the cover of *Side Effects* printed with a reproduction of the Uccello painting *S. George and the Dragon* which inspired it, "Not My Best Side", in which the dragon, the girl, and the

---

* From *Dramatic Monologue* (Methuen, 1977): a brief and helpful account of the history of the genre. Dr Sinfield also notes that the prolific use of the dramatic monologue in the Victorian era has been claimed to represent ' ... a reaction against Romantic subjectivity, a wish to move out from the person's own emotions into an objectively-perceived world.'

knight each says a self-justifying piece about it/her/himself. Many of the monologues have been located in hospitals, and again we shall notice the importance of hospitals (or "the hospital") when we consider individual volumes.

THE DETACHED OBSERVER
> We observe it ...
> ("Campsite: Maentwrog", SE)

> I am a watcher ...
> ("The Watcher" SE)

> ... I am also
> Watchman who waketh ...
> ("Confessio Amantis", WB)

> ... Such patient watchers
> Have eyes for those who watch ...
> ("The Doctor", WB)

> For those I favour are the patient men
> Who watch, who wait ...
> ("Halley's Comet, 1985-86", WB)

Poets are inevitably "observers", though some, for example W.B. Yeats and in our own day his compatriot Seamus Heaney, have sometimes hankered after a larger slice of the action. In the case of UAF, the concept of "observing" is made explicit out of self-awareness and an awareness of the inevitable role that has to be played (as in the instances I have cited above), and is also taken to various other levels — detachment, outsider-ness, balance, dispassionateness, avoidance of bias. Romanticism, in both its 18th/19th Century days and also in its more recent incarnations, at worst becomes an excuse for self-exhibition and special pleading: even the most directly and overtly autobiographical poems of UAF (and they seem to be increasing in quantity — about 17 in the most recent two volumes) eschew any kind of unseemly self-parading. If we extend the notion of the detached observer to that of Classical restraint, we shall be somewhere near the centre of many of her declared or latent preoccupations and attitudes. One of the several poems in N-V which hint at personal problems, connects in the poem with what is called 'the hard *fiat* of genes', and is quite unselfpitying, laconic, unresentful:

> ... Others speak
> Of the shining end of the tunnel. I haven't seen it.

> This is my black.
> ("Descent", N-V)

As early as "Specialist" (SE), a portrait of a self-important and in some ways repellent character, we find:

> *I am ashamed*
> *To be annoyed* by his brutal
> Rejection of delicacy ...

an overt comment which specifies his human failings and also in effect denies serious personal involvement with them. (The italics are mine: note the minimal word 'annoyed'.) Sometimes, poems about other things, or so it appears, extend into, or are revealed as, love poems; but the expression is invariably muted, understated:

> I have grown expert on your absences
> ("Queueing outside the Jeu de Paume in Light Rain",
> WB)

> You are what   I would choose
>
>   for companion in the desert. (etc.)
> ("As well as the Bible and Shakespeare ...?", N-V)

> ... the absence of you ...
> ("Chaplaincy Fell Walk", WB)

> I drop, unprepared, into one particular
> Parish, one street, one house, one you ...
> ("Homing In", WB)

But that love is a firm if sometimes understated (almost taken for granted) positive has been apparent from the first volume to the latest:

> But love is so persistent, it survives
> With no one's help ...
> ("The Watcher", SE)

> The proud, unalterable
> Eyes of love ...
> ("A Life", N-V)

U.A. Fanthorpe disavows that there has been any significant influence of Larkin on her work, but the pervasive positive of love is an interesting bond (cf. 'What will survive of us is love' in "An Arundel Tomb"). Wittgenstein was too precipitate in declaring 'Whereof we cannot speak, thereof we must be silent'. There *are* things to be said: or "observed".

TRADITION
An awareness of the past, the rooted, the inheritance by the present of what has apparently passed:

> I am permanent as the muted roar
> Of white pigeons in my barn, as the drift
> Of dry leaves in my ancient garden
> ("Owlpen Manor", SE)

> This narrow island charged with echoes
> And whispers snares me.
> ("Earthed", SE)

> They [London's lost rivers] have gone under.
> Boxed, like the magician's assistant ...

> They return spectrally after heavy rain ...
> ('Rising Damp', ST)

> ... driving south
> Down remembered roads ...
> ("London Z to A", VO)

>   ... the ancestral
> Mutter and reek. This is then, now.
> ("Looking for Jorvik", WB)

> Some unremembered ancestor handed down to me
> The practice of walking in darkness ...
> ("Descent", N-V)

> Three centuries of reticent, meticulous lives ...
> ("Friends' Meeting House, Frenchay, Bristol", N-V)

I have quoted diverse samples from each volume to suggest both how abiding has been this set of related concerns and in how many guises it appears. UAF's attitude to the past is subtle and many-sided, and it's easier to say what it isn't. It isn't, for instance, a sentimental nostalgia for what has gone at the expense of what has replaced it, as you might say characterises Larkin's seminal "Church Going". "London Z to A" (VO) is relatively undismayed about the changes that have taken place in the capital and can even register the survival of Cockney wit in shop names such as 'Den of Antiquity' and 'Just 4 U'; on the other hand "Canal: 1977" (SE) *is* scathing about the decline of a working entity to a domain for 'pleasurecraft' and 'smooth pink families'; and "The Quiet Grave" (SE) is ironical about the bowdlerisation of the folk tradition to ' ... laconic/Improper poetry improved/For the benefit of schools'. Nor are the past and its surviving features and relicts reduced to picture post cards and chocolate box decorations. Fanthorpe's churches (cf. again Larkin's in "Church Going") are not mute repositories of lost and ancient wisdom: in Montacute Church in "Soothing and Awful" (VO) the speaker is largely amused at the inarticulate comments in the visitor's book, and "St. James's Charfield" (VO) says, non-committally, ' ... What stays/Is anybody's guess'. The chapel in "Brympton d'Evercy" (SE), which seems at first to have 'consecrated air' which 'smells different' and 'perhaps/Retains a tender feeling for mankind' turns out merely to have the central heating on for Evensong! What is interesting in it are the three statues of knight 'encased/In scales like a huge salmon', lady with 'sensual' stone lips, and 'devoted eyes/Of the long priest': i.e. it is these people, not the religious significance of the place, which claim attention. Likewise, "Horticultural Show" (SE), apart from its implicit celebration of the wholesomeness of the natural world, will have none of the Larkin view in "Show Saturday" which finds that event a repository of time-honoured practices and, therefore, values. The poems in which the notions of "tradition" (not a word the poems actually employ, as a rule) in some form surface seem at pains to avoid the simplistically Romantic; and yet some notion of and feeling for the past *is* pervasive. One of the most obviously "patriotic" poems (though quite devoid of the political overtones of that word) is"Earthed" (SE), which locates roots, (though not without some local textual suggestions of resentment: 'narrow', 'snares', and as a phrase in the opening stanza declares plainly, if humorously, 'stuck in the mud'), firmly in the rural and even the rustic — there is even a trace of Prospero's enchanted isle about it. The context of many poems is certainly rural, though it *is* largely a context rather than a foreground in its own right — indeed, very little of UAF's poetry is significantly to do with the urban. At the mid-point of *Side Effects*, as well as the poems already cited, there are also other poems which deal with rural permanencies and also have picturesque names: "Stanton Drew", "Owlpen Manor", "Coire Dubh".

Perhaps the recurrent use of classical myths, legends and characters (Janus, Charon, Sisyphus, Pomona and Vertumnus, and so on) helps to point to what defines UAF's attitude to the past: it is, in an obvious and even self-evident sense I agree, but it needs to be stated, in terms of what is handed on that we are necessarily to some extent what *we* are and *things* are, and will be. I think she moralises a good deal less than, for instance and again, Larkin, or than Hughes in his different way, about the *desirability* of continuity, but she is often not content simply to record the fact of it:

"tradition" here, in the inclusive sense in which I am referring to it, is a matter of what is *real*, the kind of truth that "the real" is. In an early poem "Pat at Milking Time" (SE), the reality of the situation is not, for instance, touched with any kind of magic (as even a poem as "realistic" as Heaney's "Churning Day" is touched):

> What a field contains
> — Sun, daisies, wind — is not to be imagined ...

— because it is absolutely and irrevocably and in the case of Pat's 'sick' enterprise grimly *there*. As I said earlier, the past is not presented as a rose-coloured distortion; it concerns what has survived and is to that extent permanent:

> I remember after. And after
>
> And before, the mute persistence of water
> And grass and trees ...
> ("Canal, 1977", SE)
>
> But the trees were before. Their roots run back
> Below Grendel's forest.
> ("King Edward's Flora", N-V)

I have already said, and should stress, that there is no distorted romanticising: the repositories of 'the keys of the kingdom' of the folk song tradition, for instance, were

> Unfriendly old men in workhouses

and

> An old woman gathering stones,
> Who seized Sharp* by his gentle-
> Manly lapels, blowing her song into his mind
> Through wrinkled gums.
> ("The Quiet Grave", SE)

On the other hand, the legendary pre-Conquest and unwelcome visitors to these islands, the Vikings, whose very name is to the popular mind redolent of plunder and pillage, etc., are seen in a long and finally favourable historical perspective, adapting to tradition rather than destroying it:

* Cecil Sharp, legendary collector of folk songs.

> ... they swapped
> Languages, garments, gods. Wherever
> They settled, they conformed affably
> To the prevailing rules ...

> ... they vanished into the people
> They became, leaving their Viking selves
> Underground ...
>   ("Northmen", VO)

If I have not finally or with full coherence anatomised her many-sided attitude to "tradition", perhaps it is because she has not, finally or simply, pinned it down in a definitive way: but the past is as undeniable and pervasive as

> The hard *fiat* of genes
>   ("Descent", N-V)

In this particular poem, there is a reference (closely documented, for once, in a footnote, in order to help us to understand it exactly: with a few exceptions she mostly prefers poems to speak for themselves*. Where she doesn't, the notes are always important) to the story of one Mettus Curtius who, in effect to appease the Gods, leaped into a chasm which had appeared in the Roman forum; he is chosen in the poem by the speaker 'as ancestor' who

> Willingly entered the dark; who worked,
>   however blindly
> However strangely, for good, under the earth.
>   Who worked.
>   ("Descent", N-V)

This metaphor is closely related to a number of others to do with things underground, sometimes surfacing, though not here. Perhaps this is the way tradition "works" and the past inevitably finds its way into the present. Ultimately, of course, this "working" is to do with continuities of all kinds, with things persisting, persevering, going on ...

WORDS, WORDS:
> ... Words are my element.
> Photograph *them*.
>   ("Awkward Subject", N-V) — [*My italics but I*
>   *think implicit*]

---

* Perhaps on occasion there is *under*-footnoting: but this raises issues, finally unresolvable, which will be taken up briefly in Ch. Two.

In the beginning were the words ...
("Genesis", ST)

Some poets are more conscious of, and knowledgeable about, the basic tool of their trade, words, than others; some write more homogeneously than others, to the extent that their single-minded "voice" can be heard in pretty well all they write. (Wordsworth is a case in point, so is Browning, probably, in spite of his addiction to the dramatic monologue. You can usually hear Browning chuntering away in the background.) A discussion of "language" inevitably and quickly extends to what "language" is about, but certain extensions to earlier remarks about UAF and her use of words can be made here. I have suggested two common qualities: a more than usually wide variety, and a more than common precision — the linguistic equivalent of other kinds of precision, historical and botanical, for instance. But words exist in contexts, and true poetry manages to assemble them in the right order into "textures": which in the case of this poetry are often subtle and require a thoughtful readership. The ideal, for the poet, is to simulate spontaneity and avoid the manufactured-seeming, no matter how the words finally arrive on the paper.

To all this must be added the universal tendency to play around with words, sometimes to go so far as to fool around; to pun, to write conceits both brief and extended (indeed, sometimes pervading an entire poem — cf. the plant/Vine conceit in "Friends' Meeting House ...", N-V or "Rural Guerillas" in ST), to be witty in expected and unexpected places. The variety of language derives partly, but only partly, from the variety of speakers of dramatic monologues; the characters in 3rd-person description are also depicted in appropriate language. But amongst the monologues-proper which exhibit language characterising speakers, an obvious group is the *ONLY HERE FOR THE BIER* (ST) quartet of Shakespearian women: freely based on the originals but in three out of the four cases easily recognisable. (The fourth scarcely exists in her particular play in her own right.) The title of the group is, of course, a typical piece of irreverent fun. All the characters speak versions of the contemporary vernacular, which brings them ironically up to date; here is the opening of the mumsy Gertrude's:

> Such a nice girl. Just what I wanted
> For the boy ...
> ("Mother-in-law")

Here, in contrast, is the debby "Waiting Gentlewoman" who scarcely appears in *Macbeth*:

> If Daddy had known the setup,
> I'm absolutely positive, he'd never
> Have let me come.

In fact, UAF's use of the demotic extends as far as an "Unauthorised Version" of the St. Luke Martha/Mary/Lazarus story; here's a sample of the distinctly Liverpudlian Mary recalling the raising of Lazarus:

> ... If he'd just walked in
> When Lazzie was ill, and said, *O.K., Lazzie,*
> *You're off the sick list now* — that'd have lacked impact.
> ("Unauthorised Version", WB)

(The same poem glosses the feeding of the five thousand by 'Josh', i.e. Jesus, as 'The famous fish-butty picnic'.) This is at one end of the colloquial range; at the other (or at several others) we have these kinds of writing:

> Armour of phrase disarms despair;
> Ancestral patchwork plasters.
> ("Word Games 2 ... ", N-V)

> ... Such patient watchers
> Have eyes for those who watch.
> ("The Doctor", WB)

> Mackerel wigs dispense the justice of air.
> ("First Flight", WB)

> ... My emblems are albums,
> The bride's mother's orchid corsage, the dark cortège.
> ("Janus", ST)

These instances are, variously, terse, play with mutually-reinforcing meaning and sound, alert to linguistic possibilities at a far remove from the colloquial, concrete, graphic and precise. Quite simply, different poems seek the idiom they need: this, not a Procrustean homogeneity, is their unifying factor, if one is looking for that. What is perhaps obvious is the alertness these poems expect: for instance, there is the chime and punning in the first sample (armour/disarm/despair), the pun of 'patient' in the second (watchers of patients/watchers who are being patient). When the speaker in "The Conductor" (ST) declares, 'I am/The music's master', we should register the difference between this last phrase with its apostrophe and "music master" which measures the gap between the desirable and this person's self-estimated superiority to the music. When, in "The Passing of Alfred" (ST) (i.e. Tennyson), we read:

> We who differ, whose dears are absorbed
> Into breezy wards for routine terminations

we should note the pun on 'breezy' (and register the inappropriate attitude to dying in one of the meanings), and the deplorable gulf between the dismissive and official-sounding euphemism 'routine terminations' (and the grim resonance of 'terminations') and the actual human situation being described: in other words, the lines are laced with subtle irony. Perhaps enough has been said to illustrate the varying reader-expectations of the various poems and their varied idioms. What needs one further mention is the characteristic mingling of the serious and the various kinds of not-serious in this writing: but we are already into another pervasive feature of the poems, which must now be exemplified:

IRONIES:
     — as I have already plurally called them to suggest a range: but will now revert to the singular collective category word "irony". It is the most delicate, elusive and subtle tool of satire, as invective is the bluntest (UAF doesn't use this) and it is typical of much of the more critical of her poems, for example many of the "hospital" ones, to employ it in various degrees: sometimes, indeed, only very careful reading will determine precisely *what* degree at any one point. But before this can be done (and I'm not suggesting a long or even necessarily a conscious process, just an alert one) you need to be aware that irony is present. Sometimes, indeed, your suspicions are only confirmed retrospectively; and irony is often cumulative in degree inasmuch as each fresh example piles weight onto what precedes it. A poem which begins in this disarming way:

> These men are rich; they buy
> Pictures before asking prices ...
> ("Reception in Bristol", N-V)

might (almost?) be the opening of a poem in praise of those who put the value of art before that of cash: but the poem builds in steady, two-line shots at its target, through this at the mid-point:

> Schools that encourage music, says the chairman,
> Have no hooligans. No one replies ...

(because we are by now aware that the poem is one of restrained contempt, and maybe considerably more than this, we surmise that 'No one replies' because of the sheer daftness of the chairman's remark): and finally we have this blank condemnation of the 'Bristol' of the title:

> ... Chatterton poisoned himself in his London garret
> Rather than creep back here,

where the 'garret' points the contrast between the impoverished artist and the by-now-obvious prodigality of the men in the opening lines, whose 'shirts are exquisite' (and isn't 'exquisite' confirmed as ironical in retrospect?), and 'creep' is an antithesis of the vacuous ostentation of the occasion of the "Reception ... " (and isn't *this* word an ironical reference to Chatterton's lack of one?). I have to comment that *analysis* of such an irony is necessarily long-winded and probably tedious to read; and that here the irony is relatively plain.

Irony is, of course, one of the embodiments of "tone" (in the sense of the poet's attitude to subject), and as UAF's poetry is largely concerned with people, many of them apparently unremarkable (the truth of which judgement it is one of the self-appointed tasks of the poetry to question), it is important to gauge the degree of irony faithfully. Here is a varied case of samples: they are not entirely fair game as context is always to some extent a determining or at least influencing element in shaping response:

> It is a house of stairs. Books strain
> Alphabetically upwards. Critics sprang
> To eminence on their pages ...
> ("In the English Faculty Library, Oxford", ST)

> ... We prefer you
> To think of patients not as people, but
> Digits. That makes it much easier ....
> ("Jobdescription: Medical Records", SE)

> The trolley's rattle dispatches
> The last lover. Now we can relax
> Into illness, and reliably abstracted
> Nurses will straighten our sheets ...
> ("After Visiting Hours", SE)

> Someone from Dudley, whose writing suggests tight shoes,

> Reported *Nice and Cool*. The young entry
> Yelp their staccato approval:
> *Super! Fantastic! Jesus Lives! Ace!*
> (" 'Soothing and Awful' ", VO)

The most severe, and obvious, irony is in the second example; perhaps the most subtle (but truly there: the detached observer has registered something and is recording it) is in the third (e.g. 'reliably abstracted'); the loftiest and most scholarly is in the first (e.g. we note the human implications of 'strain' and the amusing continuation of 'upwards' in 'sprang'); and the most cattily entertaining is in the last (the 'tight shoes' detail is typical Fanthorpe fun and observation, the placing and alliteration of 'entry/Yelp' functional). But in the poetry of such an habitual ironist, irony comes in all shades and sizes:

> The headscarfed tourists in the comfy shoes
> Obediently make their scheduled pause
> Among the pigeons.
> ("The West Front At Bath", SE)

'Headscarfed' and 'comfy' characterise as well as describing, 'Obediently' is an implicit comment (these are people reduced to touristic zombies), and 'Among the pigeons' appropriately and anti-climactically locates the cultural (etc.) level of the event. But how about, in a commemorative poem not as a whole remotely ironic:

> ... Massed choirs sang solidly
> Through the masses of Haydn.
> ("My Brother's House", SE)

What about 'solidly'? And 'Through'? And 'Massed ... /... masses'? (And isn't 'masses' not merely music of a liturgical character but also a punning comment on their quantity?)

THE ORDINARY, THE EXTRAORDINARY
> ... *Lazarus, come forth!* and out comes Lazzie
> In his shroud. Well, even a halfwit could see
> Something out of the ordinary was going on.
> But this *was* just ordinary ...
> ("Unauthorised Version", WB)

> ... And thinking

> The rest of our lives, the rest of our lives
> Doing perfectly ordinary things together ...

> I hold them crammed in my arms, colossal crops
> Of shining tomorrows that may never happen ...
> ("7301", W B)

> I try to pin down the homely fact
> Of what happened, was felt.
> ("Programmed", N-V)

> ... the sustaining
> Ordinariness of things.
> ("Inside", ST)

The quotation from the *Lyrical Ballads* Preface which heads this chapter illustrates the paradox which my first two illustrations from the poems themselves illustrate: it is sharp perception embodied in appropriate language which transforms what for most of us would be 'the ordinary' into the 'extraordinary': the very ordinary words of Mary in the first quotation confront us with a paradox which cannot be resolved in her ordinary language (deriving from her ordinary perception of events); and then the poem has, by its terms of reference, to move on (not, I should add, a poem concerned with trying to come to terms with the miracle but to update a Bible story by rewriting it in contemporary language): the raising of Lazarus *was* and *was not* 'ordinary' to Mary. The first of the two quotations from "7301*" (separated, in fact, by several lines, so there is perhaps no conscious wish to point the paradox) has the phrase 'perfectly ordinary'; and we have to take 'perfectly' quite literally in this context, it is not a simple intensive: but then how can something 'ordinary' also be something "perfect"? (Indeed, the second quotation refers to a harvest of 'shining tomorrows': perfect enough.) I hope I am not making a mountain out of a molehill, but it seemed necessary to try to reconcile the notion of "ordinariness", in which UAF often seems to deal (and in several places says she deals), with the striking impression the poems have on the reader, yet why the poems also strike one as "true", faithful to common and shared experience. It's the way you re-make it in language that's the thing. Wordsworth's "Idiot Boy" remains an idiot boy, for all the poet's brief of transformation in undertaking his quota of *Lyrical Ballads*. Perhaps the model (if she existed: she does now) of UAF's college cleaner wasn't much more articulate than he was: but the character as she is presented is as wholly articulate as she needs to be to communicate her self-righteousness, scepticism, censoriousness, nosiness masquerading as charity and misanthropy as wisdom, etc.: all here in a few selected lines:

> ... These girls, mind,
> They're not all as innocent as you'd think.
> Twenty stubs in an ashtray.
>
> I can tell a lot from that.
> ("The Cleaner", VO)

So can we.

THE WITNESS BEARER:
> 'If I have any "objectives", it's to bear witness, to say, 'I have seen this, and no one else was there looking at this precise moment'.
> (U.A. Fanthorpe: Interview, Appendix B)

---

* The title is a calculation of the number of happy, shared days and of the hoped-for number of 'tomorrows' to come.

We are here to bear witness ...
We are not necessary, but we are needed.
   ("Chorus", ST)

   ... I am the witness, bound to set down
What I see.
   ("La Débâcle. Temps Gris", WB)

     ... the wildness of Vine, which exacts
Such difficult witness; whose work is done
In hopeless places ...
   ("Friends' Meeting House, ... ", N-V)

The origin of the phrase "bearing witness" is lost in the mists of forensic and ecclesiastical history: but it continues to resonate with the serious notions of responsible truth-telling, the kind of cross-my-heart absolute we believed in as children. It is a much more fundamental business than, say, the mere faithful reporting of experience; it is to do with integrity and fairness and total honesty. If the "hospital experience" so nags at the poet's memory and sensibility (in SE, ST and N-V collectively, over 30 poems derive from it), it is because it writes largely and unignorably certain truths about the relations between haves and have-nots, about the denial of human dignity, and about passing by on the other side on the part of those whose very raison d'être is to do exactly the opposite. The poetry of U.A. Fanthorpe does not, on the whole, deal with the distressing details of contemporary national and world events, and crises of unemployment, urban decay, rising crime, the insolence of political office, wars, famines, and so on; though she is well aware of

   ... hopeless places, prisons, workhouses,
In counting houses of respectable merchants,
In barracks, collieries, sweatshops, in hovels
Of driven and desperate men ...
   ("Friends' Meeting House ...", N-V)

— the sprinkling of words not precisely contemporary — 'counting houses', 'merchants', 'hovels' — suggest that the problems are inherited. The following poem in this sequence of three, in matching 18th Century language, "The Middle Passage", has a Barry Unsworth-like awareness (cf. *Sacred Hunger*) of the degradation aboard the 18th Century 'slavers' and of the unwholesomeness of the part played in Bristol in their transactions by, e.g., 'respectable merchants'. But on the whole, what this poetry does concern itself with is the underlying permanencies, particularly of people, with their inheritance, their significant individuality and their fraught and fragile relationships, lived out in a world endlessly interesting, where living out is possible, trying to make enough sense of it, sometimes being pathetic or failures or unappealing but managing at least to "stand to". And the role of the poet?

> I was set here
> To watch. So I do,
> And report, in cipher, to headquarters,
> Which is an hypothesis.
>   ("Standing To", ST)

In other words, if 'headquarters' is 'an hypothesis', the task is nevertheless to be done. Small wonder (cf. the Interview) that U.A. Fanthorpe believes poets and poetry to have significance in the contemporary world; I hope this chapter has gone some way towards "deciphering" her priorities.

Chapter Two: From *Side Effects* to *Neck-Verse*

Side Effects (1978)

seems in retrospect to have been a particularly lively, varied and attractive first volume. In the light of what has followed, it seems to have established some thematic preferences and stylistic practices that have remained. There are three identifiable groups of poems (not that all the poems fit into such a critic's Procrustean scheme): those concerned with or stemming from experience in hospital (which I shall during the course of the chapter call "hospital" poems, and to which I shall add "From the Remand Centre", a poem about exotically-named, rejected Koreen); poems concerned with the past and "traditional" matters; and several poems apparently relating personal experiences, some satiric, for instance "Staff Party", and the two church poems. There are also some strange fantasy or dream poems, for instance "Family Entertainment", in which the speaker witnesses a spectacular fire at a large house as one of an audience; and another poem, difficult to categorise, but because of the power of its imagery I shall mention at this point, "Only a Small Death", in which the painful process of moving house is compared, in an extended and vivid conceit, with the process of a sudden death and its funereal aftermath. Several other poems, too, have an undercurrent of the ominous and of foreboding. I shall illustrate this last-named strand in the writing first, because the number of poems in which it appears is small enough to be overlooked but significant enough to be noticed. There is indeed a dark side to the poet's talent which manifests itself from time to time, not that it casts a shadow over the rest: but it's there. Here is a selection of passages to which I respond in the way I have described

> ... but no one's here of course,
> Except a sexless, ageless, shapeless shape,
> Hunched underneath the cedar ...
>
> Dramatist to this house is Death. Austere,
> Withdrawn, the scripts he writes.
> ("Ridge House [Old People's Home]")
>
> Ashy carpet flakes over sills,
> Torches wink in bedrooms, the intercom
> Mutters away to itself. A hose leaks,
> A neighbour runs past with a basin
> And towels.
> ("Family Entertainment")
>
> Never again will you sleep in
> This room, see sun rise through glass at this
> Familiar angle ...

You have died suddenly ...
    ("Only a Small Death")

Someone was dying upstairs in a slow
Damp-sheeted bed. The garden had turned strange.
The smell of its depression filtered through
Cracks in the window frames.
    ("Some Modernisation Needed")

Disturbing writing in a volume otherwise so buoyant and secure-footed. The vein, or something akin to it, appears in some quantity in *Standing To* and in *Neck-Verse*, where it will receive more detailed comment. The concreteness and particularity with which the passages I have quoted are made vivid is characteristic of the writing as a whole; one of the features of this volume which was widely acclaimed was its fidelity to the "real" world, and no group of poems in UAF's entire body of work has a better claim to this quality than the "hospital" group, with its cast of the lowly, the humble, the "disadvantaged' in one way or another. ("The Watcher" and "Patience Strong" are not obviously of this group but are in fact "hospital" poems).

    The situation is that of a clerk/typist working in a hospital (I shall treat the poems as poems, not as the autobiography I know them in a general way to be, and I will return to this topic in some detail later). This clerk, sometimes narrator, sometimes observer/presenter, records the activities of an institution in which the inmates, the 'Handicapped, handcuffed, unhandy,/Muddled, moribund, mute' ("The List") are in one way or another mistreated by a System in which power structures, incompetence and priorities reduce them to ciphers and statistics. UAF does not overtly make the connection with what has been happening in Britain's Systems as a whole in recent years, and one should not wish to see the poems' concerns as equivalent to those of *Guardian* leader and letter writers: but to anyone who has lived through these years, the wider connections will not have to be argued overmuch. They make in this respect an interesting comparison with, say, Larkin's "The Building", which is never named and in which a wider resonance likewise enlarges the scope of the poem. The sense of offence, pity or compassion is in the selection of detail, sometimes in the irony, rather than, on the whole, in overt comment: but abstaining from this is a poetic strategy, not euphemism, as the positives of the volume — affection, caring, sympathy, understanding, being properly and decently civilised, being humane — everywhere affirm. No two "hospital" poems cover the same ground in the same way, so the poems are not, as sometimes happens in volumes with persistent concerns, versions of each other. Thus, the opening poem, "The List", which puts down a marker for the rest, illustrates how typing lists of names is a kind of parodic reduction to 'tranquil order' of the various "incompetents" (my word, not the poem's) who people the other poems, and resurface in some quantity in *Standing To* and *Neck-Verse*. The extended conceit in which the items are compared with the 'pacers' who are 'giftbearers in a frieze' along 'the Valley of the Kings' is ironic: nothing could be further from such 'harmonious' procession than the reality of those to whom the 'list' relates, those 'stained by living', as they are described. (The relevance of the Egyptian cover of the Penguin *Selected Poems* is not limited to this: the British Museum item of which the cover is a reproduction is called, to give it its full title — partly omitted on the cover itself — "The Weighing of the Heart of the Scribe Ani against the Feather of Truth". The point is that the hospital-scribe, who is also the poet-scribe, cares deeply about the "truth" being recorded in these poems.) The poem seems dispassionate, but the 'list' of the fourth verse, which I have already quoted, sets out the stall of these poems' concerns. "Jobdescription: Medical Records" is perhaps the most damning of the series: the System explains itself this way:

> ... We do not encourage
>
> Speculation in clerks. We prefer you
> To think of patients not as people, but
> Digits. That makes it easier.

'Digits' is more loftily dismissive than, say, "numbers", and has sound-and line-placing emphasis. The language of much of the poem is impersonal officialese, and the System is the speaker, so the poem can only comment by selection of detail, as happens in other poems of the series. "Specialist" is the first poem we have encountered in which the speaker's second thoughts modify her initial ones (cf. in this volume "Patience Strong", and in ST, "A Gardener"). At the outset, the specialist is depicted in unmistakably satiric terms ('Ichor' here is the ethereal fluid believed to fill the veins of the Gods):

> This specialist
> Holds himself upright lest
> He spill a drop of his precious
> Ichor.
>
> Rose-cheeked, dwarf-high ...

Yet he soon appears as quite other than ridiculous:

> He is brave with
> Convicted murderers, female
> Thugs, aggressive juveniles ...

But even this is not the entire story of his complex set of attributes: this verse continues

> ... but
> Dare not
>
> Raise his eyes when
> His inferiors cross his path.

He is like a captain of a dinghy in which there is 'no space ... for/Subordinates', he has a 'fog-horn' voice. The penultimate verse has already been quoted in Ch. One in another connection; here we should note the speaker's overt self-criticism: but (and I will quote the verse again in a moment) it is unexpected for what I called in Ch. One the "minimal" 'annoyed' to be followed by 'brutal rejection', and 'ashamed' seems a very strong recantation of some of what has preceded it:

> I am ashamed
> To be annoyed by his brutal
> Rejection of delicacy ...

But he does, after all, give so much of himself: yet we note the continuation of the satiric terminology in which this redeeming quality is expressed: he

> Pours out so much
> Of his ichor, modulates so
> Touchingly his loud-hailer, for
> His landsick patients.

An interesting poem in which praise and blame are finely balanced.

The two "Casehistories ... " of Julie and Alison (the reductive labelling word in the poems' titles is the System's) offer examples of the kind of pathos which are not the System's concern. In the case of Julie, ironically-interspersed quotations from *Hamlet* about Ophelia lend some dignity to the minimal verse of Julie's sad, mad monologue (the full title of the poem is "Casehistory: Julie (encephalitis)"):

> I'm getting better,
> The doctor told me so,
> As God's me witness, touch wood.
> O, I am hungry.
> I hope you don't mind me asking,
> Where's the toilet to?

Do you see this, O God?

This last question, Laertes' anguished response to the madness of Ophelia, is the poem's final, devastatingly-ironical and open-ended quotation: Julie is clearly not going to "get better", no matter what the doctor said. Presumably he knows this too: some of these dramatic monologues suggest many things between their lines, as do speeches in plays. Alison's poem ("Casehistory: Alison (head injury)") is a contrasting monologue of a once 'bright girl' looking mutely and unrecognisingly at a photograph of herself when she was someone whose

> ...... autocratic knee
>
> Like a Degas dancer's
> Adjusts to the observer with airy poise,

the knee which now, in pathetic contrast, 'lugs me upstairs/Hardly' (and we register both senses of this last word). The poem consists of the unspoken thoughts of Alison: a different and ingenious kind of dramatic monologue in which the speaker bows out and allows Alison's thoughts, as she contemplates her former "unbroken face", to emerge in reverie, with not a few reminders that she still retains some semblances of the 'bright girl' in her thinking and her responses. The pathos is in the contrast between her past and present selves (both there in the poem), not in any overt comment (for the monologue cannot allow this); and there is (again, the mode of presentation, the circumstances of the event, do not permit it) no self-pity, just mute observation as she 'looks at her photograph', as the note below the title explains.

> Her face, broken
> By nothing sharper than smiles, holds in its smiles
> What I have forgotten ...

'Her face' is the face in the photograph of her former self, now a total stranger to her and, unlike the face of the present version of herself, or so the poem suggests, not 'broken' by the injury she suffered. Even 'holds' is suggestive — of both the hands that "hold" the photograph and of the past world that the photograph silently contains as a permanency.

Perhaps I could, as a digression, further illustrate the ingenuity in some of the poems in this volume by some consideration (not a detailed analysis: in fact throughout, I shall have no space to do more than comment on details and portions) of what is perhaps UAF's best-known poem, "Not My Best Side", happily, at Harry Chambers' instigation, printed on the cover below a reproduction of the Uccello painting "*S. George and the Dragon*" which inspired it. It too is ingeniously devised and has an immediate appeal yet fits into none of the categories I devised for the volume at the outset: so much for critical simplifications. The three speakers, the Dragon, the Lady and St. George, not only reveal characters which are both possible versions of themselves as Uccello paints them, and also grow and develop in their new verbal dimension as the idioms of their speeches propel them into the contemporary world (so St. George is a kind of efficient, bullying technocrat and the Lady is a mock-innocent, finally prudential minx), but the three of them also comment on each other: so the Dragon's humorously-resigned version of himself is quite different from the Lady's perception of his 'lovely green skin and that sexy tail'. (And yes, there it is in the picture.)

The group of poems which I have associated with "tradition", with the rural past and its ways, bears out in detail what has been outlined in general terms in Ch. One. I now wish to discuss at greater length the attitudes inherent and implicit in these poems' depiction of the essentially rural. To what extent is it not merely "old", and by its very abidingness to be — what? Respected? Or merely noted as "there for a long time"? Are there other ingredients, is there an outcrop of "the picturesque" (I have already noted the disavowal of chocolate-box-cover Nature, but I have also registered the undeniable attractiveness of some of the place names: Owlpen Manor, Brympton d'Evercy, and so on). Not a simple issue, and certainly connected with the matter of Classical/Romantic raised in Ch. One. It also concerns the value which the poetry gives to the "permanent", as it is embodied in places, buildings and landscapes.

Deep waters; but they must be navigated if we are to explore some of these poems' constant positives. I shall present a further selection of quotations (and repeat for convenience one made before), and then consider their implications. Before that, we should note a specific dismissal of the world of the chocolate-box cover:

> ... Trite calenders
> Of rose-nooked cottages or winding ways ...
>
> Characteristic cottage gardens, seen
> Through chintzy casement windows ...
> ("Patience Strong", SE)

So if the bogus, clichéd and prettified are rejected, what is celebrated? I number the samples for convenient reference:

> (1)   ... the chalky
> Kent mud, thin sharp ridges between wheel-tracks, in
> Surrey's wild gravel,

In serious Cotswold uplands ...
("Earthed")

(2)   ... these stones,
Pitted and unemphatic ...
They are the most permanent
Presences here ...
                    ... Put
Your hand on stone. Listen
To the past's long pulse.
("Stanton Drew")

(3)   We are what they achieved. The hay
Raked, hedges laid, milk scoured, rats
Trapped, eels skinned, clothes scrubbed, earth
Dug by these laborious tools ...
("Brympton d'Evercy: 1. The Priest's House")

(4)   The river's hollow comment ...
                    ... these acres
Of glowing uneloquent water ...

You, who are looked for, are the ones
Who are not here ...
We tramp where you should live

In your jolly squalid hovels ...
("Coire Dubh")

(5)   Who cared for the kingdom?
An old woman gathering stones,
Who seized Sharp by his gentle-
Manly lapels, blowing her song into his mind
Through wrinkled gums ...
("The Quiet Grave")

(6)   The wood was a real wood, and
You could get lost in it. The trees
Had no names or numbers.
("My Brother's House")

(7)   ... the pocky stonework
Ruining mildly in mottled silence,
The gutted pub, the dropping sounds
Inside the tunnel ...

> ... the picturesque antiquity
> That savaged so many who made it.
> ("Canal: 1977")

(8) They visit hidden places of the earth
     When tenderly with fork and hand they grope
     To lift potatoes, and the round, flushed globes
     Tumble like pearls out of the moving soil.
     ("Men on Allotments")

Some glossing might be helpful. In (3), 'we' are literally "we", and 'they' are the rustic tools once used by the peasants, now exhibited in the priest's house. In (4), 'you' are those exiled from the place (the Scottish Highlands). In (5), 'Sharp' is Cecil Sharp, the dedicatee of the poem, the celebrated collector of folk songs and pioneer preserver of this country's folk-song tradition. In (6), the contrast is between a "natural" wood and one created by, e.g. the Forestry Commission (not named, but implicit). Basically, the rural is a place to live in and be in and do appropriate and useful things in. It goes back and back and is unpretentious, honest, solid, wholesome, not superficially beautiful (not ugly either: but UAF isn't really concerned with aesthetics here): 'picturesque' in (7) is, in view of 'savaged' in the following line, at least in part ironic (or at least not unqualified). But it has endured and sustains. In (8), the allotment holders, who live on a council house estate, seem to be reaching out towards something fundamental and basic — as "visitors" yes, but in worthwhile connection with something precious (not necessarily *consciously* realised by them: the poem isn't concerned with this one way or the other). In the quotation, 'moving' is a little more than merely physical, but the poem is prepared to do no more than hint here: 'like pearls' is certainly more than a visual comparison. Elsewhere in the poem, vegetable growth is 'casual holiness' and beans 'subtle benediction': UAF's overt commitments do not usually go as far as this.

Has it, then, this rurality where "tradition" roots, nothing at all to do with the picturesque? We note that the water in (4) if 'uneloquent' is also 'glowing': not merely a matter of light but also of quality, surely? And what is "real" about a 'real' wood, i.e. what's so good about the fact that it "just growed"? I have taken the topic as far as I need, for the moment.

What I have called a "personal" group of poems in *Side Effects*, poems which are apparently autobiographical, poems relating experiences, such as "Carol Concert" and "Horticultural Show", one or two eavesdroppings on private thoughts and feelings, such as "The Watcher" and "Only a Small Death", make up the tally of the poems in the volume. The kind of honesty, lively-mindedness, wit, precision and sharp observation in the other poems are found here too. UAF has always, beginning with those in this book, written "personal" poems that are apparently autobiographical; here, as elsewhere, such poems are scarcely really intimate, are certainly not of the more embarrassingly-involving "confessional" kind, the kind which 'encouraged in the reading public a romantic confusion between poetic excellence and inner torment' (as Chris Baldick puts it in his *Concise Oxford Dictionary of Literary Terms*). They are invariably both restrained, even when concerned with an apparently close relationship, and more about what is observed than the observer: "The Watcher" seems to be putting its cards frankly on the table in a more than usually confessional way, but the 'I' of the poem is more concerned with the nature of what is "watched" and the process of "watching" than with the "watching" self. I have already declared a strong personal preference for treating apparently or even avowedly autobiographical poetry as poetry not as autobiography, and should explain further: seeing that many of UAF'S poems *are* of this kind, how to approach them is a real issue. (It would, for instance, be absurd to read the entire significant *opera* of Wordsworth, which is perhaps peculiarly autobiographical, in order to have the insights into his "self" that it offers because these will give you insights into the poetry ... If all you have are quasi-insights into the "self", the poetry is rated, if at all, by the quantity of these offered). The personal poems, both specifically autobiographical and more broadly experiential, in *this* volume do not say, "Look at me", "Involve yourself with me", but rather, "Share with me what I am observing and experiencing". Poems of this kind here are never so idiosyncratic as to merely document the wholly private observations of the self with no further relevance or "application" other than to the self: they create their own invariably concrete and realistic universalities. "My Brother's House" is one of the most attractive, and also one of the most elusive if one combs it for concrete evidence of the expected sense of loss, nostalgia and affection for something valuable which has gone. The affection and nostalgia remain implicit in the wealth of sharp detail which draws you into the house and its blend of the homely, the eccentric and the humorous, the real and unpretentious. The final summary understatement

> ... I regret the passing
> Of my brother's house. It was like living in Rome
> Before the barbarians

is, indeed, a mighty compliment, and 'barbarians' a rebarbative entity in the context of the poem and indeed of the volume. The term "civilised", if I apply it to the writing of UAF here and elsewhere, does not encompass the "genteel" but the "real", the "sound, because tried and tested". Add to this what was said earlier about "tradition" and the desirable and undesirable behaviour exhibited in the "hospital" poems, and a set of related positives emerges. As for the gatherings depicted in "Carol Concert", "Rite" and "Staff Party", if they are unseemly they can expect to be satirised:

> ... an impromptu hilarious
> Madrigal group (three beards and one
> Long skirt) intone delicately ...
>> ("Rite")

> These sculptured hairdos, these fairy-
> Tale dresses, gothic embraces —
> *Sophie, long time no see !*
>> ("Carol Concert")

> Silky and bland, like Roman emperors,
> With kiss curls trained across their noble brows,
> They sit, my colleagues ...
>> ("Staff Party")

Sharply-observed, "what-oft-was-thought" writing, and the targets are familiar, fair game. It is, as always, the detail that is telling: the artiness of the members of the madrigal quartet (and one of them must be a counter-tenor), the apposite décor of 'sculptured' and 'gothic', and the daft customary greeting, and 'trained' in the final sample (these *are* teachers!). In view of the manifold absurdities of our time, there is perhaps less poetry satire about than you would expect; Fanthorpe's is amongst the most notable.

Standing To (1982).

The second volume is the longest of the five, but did not (as sometimes happens) mop up a tally of poems "left over" from *Side Effects*. It would be easy to say, and hard to demonstrate, that it is "more assured", "extends her range" and so on — the kind of thing reviewers often say and sometimes get away with. Certainly the number of pure dramatic monologues has increased (to about a dozen in a total of something over fifty), and certainly their range could scarcely be greater: from Jesus Christ to a mentally-handicapped hospital patient. Subtitles in the volume try to organise the contents in groups, but I don't think they would be particularly helpful for my summary comments: I shall rely on impressions and say that there are many references to death and the dead, as well as (again) to the dispossessed (there are about a dozen "hospital" poems); and, paradoxically, a pervasive zest, wit and, again, what I can only call "sharpness". The impression the volume leaves is neither negative nor depressing, though a catalogue of its subjects, again largely people, would scarcely be cheerful. "Standing To", explains a cover quotation from U.A.F.'s words in an article by Diana Hendry in *Gloucestershire and Avon Life*, is (I paraphase) a soldier's condition of readiness for action and unexpected eventualities. The title of the volume, indeed like at least four of the five titles, suggests a kind of obliqueness to the actual processes of living (which writing, as I said in the previous chapter, inevitably entails but which this writing seems to be quite concious of). Apart from the title poem and "The Constant Tin Soldier", where you would expect it, there's an unusual amount of military imagery in the book (everywhere in "Fanfare", for instance, and surprisingly in "At Cadbury" and "Haunted House"). Perhaps being brought up in the Second World War drove such imagery deep into the subconscious of those who were young and impressionable and had to live through it. I don't, in short, find any further significance in the fact, but other readers might wish to do so. There seems also to be an even greater overall complexity and sheer ingenuity of theme and execution, notably, for instance, in such poems as "Inside", "Janus", "Prolepsis" and "The Conductor". But many poems are less technically arresting than these, yet in their way no less effective (in other words, technical virtuosity is not to be equated with exclusive merit); nevertheless, a "standing to" state of alertness is once again invariably called for in the reader. As a final generalisation, and indeed this applies to other volumes too, there is a constant attempt to discover the truth under appearance, "being" concealed by "seeming". "Inside" makes the point in a stark and uncompromising way:

> Inside our coloured, brisk world,
> Like a bone inside a leg, lies
> The world of the negative. ...
>
> Suddenly the immense and venerable
> Fallacies that prop the universe
> Fail ...

Apart from the suggestion of X-rays in one of the meanings of the pun 'negative' and its contextual place in the volume's "hospital" group, the poem is no more about the interior of a hospital than, say, Larkin's "The Building" is limited in significance to the hospital it never names. Similarly, "Rising Damp", ostensibly about how the 'little fervent underground/Rivers of London',

> *Effra, Graveney, Falcon, Quaggy,*
> *Wandle, Walbrook, Tyburn, Fleet,*

with their names picturesquely redolent of their natures and their place in history, and which surface unstoppably after heavy rain, 'Confounding suburban gardens', contrast with the more sinister rivers of classical mythology, which 'lie/Lower', 'touch us only in dreams', and 'never surface': the poem suggests at the symbolic level (which is its true provenance) the way "tradition" works, the workings of the mind, hidden fears of death, and so on. In another poem, "At the Ferry", Charon waits on the bank of his river as death waits on life. The gardener from 'the Funny Farm', who appears to have no particular expertise to offer the world, turns out to be an expert with trees and plants ("A Gardener") and confounds the speaker's initial estimate of him: this kind of *volte-face* is a recurrent feature of many of Fanthorpe's poems — but no such miscalculation is made about 'the instantly forgotten patients' of "Lament for the Patients": though they *seem* to be so, the detailed commemoration in the poem ensures that they are not so. "Getting it across" is also, in one sense, about the truth of "being" under "seeming": the Son of Man Himself, who provokes 'jaw-cracking yawns' in His disciples with endless and repeated stories and parables, is concerned with the utterly serious business of writing the truth 'on flesh', their flesh; and 'Pete'

> with his headband stuffed with fishooks

and all the others, unpromising for such a role as they might superficially seem to be, are in reality

> ... my medium. I called them.

The constant updating of the idiom to the contemporary in this and other poems which deal in the past (e.g. the four Shakespearian monologues, "Sisyphus", "Pomona and Vertumnus") is a mode of revealing permanent truth underlying the seeming particularity of past events: "being" under "seeming". It is no paradox, and should not be surprising, that a poet so precisely aware of the details of the historical past where it touches her poetry should in this way reveal the relevance of the past to the present, and thus of the present as a living embodiment of the past: which is an elaborate way of saying how an awareness of the fructifying influence of "tradition" pervades the poetry in several complementary ways.

I shall concentrate most of my more detailed comments on some of the poems in two notable groups, "hospital" and "dramatic monologues", which include some of the most striking in the collection. As in the case of the "hospital" poems in *Side Effects*, no two poems of the genre here cover the same ground or in other ways duplicate each other. One of the most elaborate is "The Conductor"; the eponymous central figure conducting a symphony of life and death on an 'orchestra' of the senile, the epileptic, and the rest of the human casualties over whom 'I preside' (the imperiously-aloof word characterises the attitude), is 'the receptionist' of the penultimate verse. His/her (the sex is undetermined even by 'I shoot my cuffs' in the penultimate verse) dictatorial control seems arrogant above his/her station and true role, indeed almost God-usurping: s/he, in turn, is at the end of the poem displaced by Hermes, the messenger of Zeus himself. S/he is one of the addicts of power who appear amongst the top echelons of UAF's "hospital world": remote from the patients 'dribbling urine and spittle' to the extent that s/he can speak of them (the poem *is* a dramatic monologue, with a possible intervention at the end as 'A new conductor,/Young, fetching, shifty, immortal', in fact 'Hermes who leads men's souls in another direction', makes his mysterious entrance) in a way which is both witty in itself and critical of him/her:

> Depression's largo, schizophrenia's scherzo ...

> The plagal cadence of the stretcher-borne dying ...

We are entertained by the conceit as it is worked out, and yet aware, in the way that poetry contrives to have it both ways, of the offensively inappropriate attitude to the objects of the wit. The elaborately contrived conceit of conductor/receptionist:orchestra/patients strikes a new technical chord in the "hospital" writing; but, as we shall notice in other examples, the conceit in both its extended and incidental forms is a *favourite* device.

Other poems too extend the range of the "hospital" genre: the nightmarish world of "Inside" has already been touched upon in a discussion of themes, and must now be examined in more detail. It is perhaps the most negative poem in the entire *opera*, the rock-bottom revelation of the stark truth of the barebones of being under the seemings and deceptions of the world of the 'sustaining/Ordinariness of things', in which

>   ... the immense and venerable
> Fallacies that prop the universe
> Fail ...

It is, we note, a linguistic inevitability for 'Fallacies' to 'Fail', and the two line-beginnings and heavy alliterative emphasis underline this truth. The poem is all the more powerful for its brutal concrete particularity:

>   ... Here the blood
> Screams whispers to the flesh.

The collision of contradictions ('Screams whispers') enacts the collision of the surface and deep-down worlds which result in demoralisation and confusion; this is a land in which 'the alien wanders/Endless benighted streets', isolated in suffering from the world of the ordinary where 'innocent households ... believe in tomorrow'. No such belief in *this* poem.

Perhaps even more graphic is "Prolepsis". A prolepsis is an anticipation — here of 'Death at a stroke' (the pun refers both to the instant in time and the affliction). The extended conceit in the poem compares the way the producer uses make-up to simulate age in the young actor and how the 'new producer', the stroke, makes her literally age by touching her head:

> One hemisphere's sure pilot faltered,
> Brain's tempo altered.

(We should register how, in this poem, meaning is sharpened by rhyme, punching at the ends of short lines.) After that, the distortion of make-up to "rehearse" age on a young face to produce

> Mouth's drag, the florid swag
> Of flesh round socket, cheekbone, chin.
> The writing on the skin

is no longer needed.

I have already mentioned "A Gardener" and "Not Quite Right": more orthodox UAF territory, with their redemption of the humble. (It is difficult to pitch this noun, which implies a judgement the poet does not make.) Another poem, "Resuscitation Team", is a dramatic narrative, with a degree of critical implication, depicting a (failed) attempt to revive a woman who has had a heart attack: the entire procedure, until the corpse is abandoned by the team which 'Leaves at the double' in quest of the next task, is undertaken with the rowdy horseplay of detached professionalism in which, ironically but inevitably

> ... The indifferent patient

> Is not amused, but carries little weight.

After that, the corpse ('If she is a corpse') is abandoned and

> ... One of us,
> Uncertainly, rearranges the nightdress.

— 'the', not 'her' which is no longer appropriate. A longer poem, one that might stand as typifying in these "hospital" poems the deploring of the treatment of patients as ciphers rather than as humans, and one that celebrates the utterly rock-bottom "ordinary", is "Lament for the Patients". Where "Prolepsis" is terse, this poem is more discursive; and like all the rest of the poems of the genre, it eschews facile pity or sympathy:

what there is of these two essential positives is embodied in the simple, unsentimental roll call which occurs towards the end of the poem:

> These I remember:
> Sonia, David, Penny, who chose death.
> Lynn and Gillian, who died undiagnosed.
> Peter, whose death was enigmatic.
> Simple Betty, who suddenly stopped living.

Thus far the extent of their human significance — but their mere names and modes of dying differentiate and dignify them; we note the (as I read it) euphemism of the second line, in which the expression 'chose death' functions as a delicate version of deliberate personal intervention.

Finally, I turn to some of the other dramatic monologues proper. The four Shakespearian portraits which comprise the fun-entitled *ONLY HERE FOR THE BIER* section are amongst the most entertaining in the volume. 'I was interested to see how the masculine world of Shakespeare's tragedies would look from the woman's angle', UAF writes in a prefatory note to the four, suggesting a view, not uncommon amongst poets, about poetry writing as a way of exploring rather than of stating preconceptions; also with some ironic disingenuousness in view of the fact that what we have (in at least two cases; and the "Waiting gentlewoman" doesn't significantly exist in the play except as a bit-part player in one scene) are to some extent variations on the plays' characters rather than pedantically-scholarly reconstructions; fleshed-out characters which exist at least in part in their own autonomous right, and some of the entertainment derives from this very counterpointing of Shakespeare's women and UAF's versions. So the rather stupid Gertrude quite misreads the Hamlet-Ophelia-Polonius situations ('Such a nice girl ... dear old fellow'), and Emilia becomes a real and blasé army wife. The ruthless, cut-and-dried Regan *is* closer to her origins, inasmuch as she exists in *King Lear* as a distinctive character: she certainly does here. The idioms of all the four women are updated to different versions of the contemporary: Regan's is clinically impersonal, ironically unfeminine:

> ... One must object, however,
> To the impropriety of those who propose
> Different rules. One is no innovator:
> Innovation is unfeminine.

This is quite distinct from the I've-seen-it-all-dear of Emilia:

> It's the place, I think. Everyone seems
> To have gone to pieces here. Oh, not me,
> My dear. I'm so used to the life. Just
> Dump me down anywhere ...

Part of the fun, of course, is in picking up references to the plays as they are seen through all those partial eyes. Here is Macbeth as the debby "Waiting gentlewoman", over whose green head it has all gone, inevitably sees him:

> ... I think
> He's gruesome. What HM sees in him
> I cannot imagine. *And* he talks to himself.
> That's so rude, I always think.

UAF palpably enjoys the irreverence of treating The Bard in this way: but someone who presents Christ as she does in "Getting it Across" is well able to have a little sport with Will. Certainly one factor in the popularity of Fanthorpe's poetry is this very refusal to be stuffy or pompous or "proper", its mischievous snook-cocking; so that when its updating turns serious (as it does in "Getting it Across") we do take it seriously: as Christ says of his disciples:

> Dying ridiculous and undignified,
> Flayed and stoned and crucified upside down,
> They are the dear, the human, the dense, for whom
> My message is.

"Irreverence" is a crude word to describe the attitude implicit in some of the writing, and I have only used it because neither I nor Roget can think of a better: the element of disrespect the word connotes is certainly not present here or elsewhere.

Three further dramatic monologues which give contemporary versions of classical myths and legends, "Janus", "Sisyphus", and "Pomona and Vertumnus", are amongst the most interesting poems in the collection: but before we notice these, we should debate what UAF's many classical references in this and other volumes signify and what they don't. It is almost inevitable in post-Freudian and post-Jungian days to expect classical references to embody archetypes, perennial psychological truths, and so on. I think UAF mostly doesn't go in for this kind of extension, though each of the stories and references has to be considered in and for itself. (And they are not all dramatic monologues: "At the Ferry", the Charon poem, for instance: though it will be convenient to mention it here in conjunction with the classical-based dramatic monologues.) I don't, therefore, feel inclined to regard "Sisyphus", in spite of its Camus epigraph, as *much* more than a vivid contemporary realisation of a fascinating and fearsome myth (even though underlying many of UAF's poems *is* the implication that life can be tough and uncompromising). This is the kind of concrete detail with which the Sisyphus story is presented:

> ... I know its [the stone's] every wart, its ribby ridges,
> Its snags, its lips. And the stone knows me,
> Cheek, chin and shoulders, elbow, groin, shin, toe,
> Muscle, bone, cartilage ...

Sisyphus *would* be vividly aware, if you are looking at things from his point of view, of his every needful muscle and physical attribute, and would think (because he fully realises the implications of his situation),

> ... The hill
> Is hostile to the stone and me.
> The stone resents me and the hill.

I have no impulse to "translate" these details into precise equivalent contemporary futilities but rather to participate in the carefully-realised psychology of a Sisyphus uniquely condemmed to such eternal long-suffering: in other words, I do not see the world of UAF as Sisyphus sees it. Likewise, I think "Pomona and Vertumnus" is largely a celebration of lively fecundity ('the Bramleys' branches/Bow with their burly cargo', etc.), and "Janus" a rarely-playful series of one-off variations on the theme of time and contrast; Janus is the versatile presiding spirit of odd temporal juxtapositions, contradictions and complementaries:

> I am director of the forgotten fiesta.
> I know why men at Bacup black their faces;

He is the other side of the coin from Vertumnus. (In the legend, Vertumnus, the finally successful suitor of Pomona, the nymph who cared for fruits and orchards, disguised himself as an old woman in order to succeed where others had failed.) Janus, in his poem, says,

> I am the future's overseer, the past's master

(characteristic word-play on "past master"); but Vertumnus says the opposite:

> ... I am the irrepressible, irresponsible
> Spirit of Now: no constant past,
> No predictable future.

I do not think the two poems are inviting me to reconcile such contrarieties into some coherent "philosophy", but rather to enjoy the re-working of classical stories, in various ways, for the contemporary reader: the poems don't merely recount, but make the stories approachable for today's non-classically-versed readership. Likewise, Charon, in "At the

Ferry", a poem in the commemorative *STATIONS UNDERGROUND* section (the title perhaps conflates "Stations of the Cross" and the "Tube" underground) is a personified version of the universal awareness of the presence of death or its messenger (just as "Prolepsis" expresses a more fearful awareness): Charon sometimes arrives to perform his customary duty of taking the dead across his river, and sometimes he is just sensed as a presence; in this personal instance, he is actually glimpsed:

> I saw you once, boatman, lean by your punt-pole
> On an Oxford river, in the dubious light
> Between willow and water ...

"At the Ferry" is a haunted, haunting poem. I have finally, in my somewhat diversified and interrupted remarks on this volume's dramatic monologues, to mention the final two poems, "The Constant Tin Soldier", and "Standing To". I have already referred to and quoted from the latter: it fairly embodies one of the volume's concerns, alert watchfulness — but, it has also to be said, creates a credible soldier character in a weirdly-eternal-seeming, Kafka-like war, but without some of the vague and mysterious features of Kafka's world: this one is clearly located in the Second World War with its 'camouflage' and other 'martial paraphernalia' — in other words, it is not simply an autobiographical poem in disguise. "The Constant Tin Soldier" is the longest poem in the book, in fact the longest published poem to date. Penguin felt it was sufficiently significant to call for its inclusion in *Selected Poems*, in spite of what was presumably a pressure on available space, so some detailed comment seems called for. If I associate this poem with, for instance, David Jones's "In Parenthesis", Pound's "Hugh Selwyn Mauberley", and, more recently, Geoffrey Hill's "The Mystery of the Charity of Charles Péguy", I merely wish to suggest its stable-mates rather than its precise content and significance. It is the history of one man, in Part 1 a soldier, in Part 2 the civilian he became, from one day late in the First War when the Germans launched a Spring Offensive, to old age in 'a five-star/Scottish hydro'; a story of survival, but also of degeneration, decline, and personal damage. He is, at the end of the poem, 'still standing to', but in the aftermath of war is diminished. (The implication of the poem, taken at its widest, is perhaps to do with the blight of war, focusing on this exemplar.) The second verse of the poem is predictive:

> It isn't always lucky to stay alive.
> Some never recover from surviving.

He seems to be one such; to say his decline is "unheroic" is scarcely appropriate if we examine the depiction of the war in Part 1 (whose sub-title recalls the famous poem of Isaac Rosenberg, "Break of Day in the

Trenches"):

> ... It rained noise,
> Mud, bone, hot lumps of jagged metal,
> Gas, smoke, fear, darkness, dissolution ...
> Across the broken earth, the broken men.

The atmosphere of the war is precisely caught in the stark detail; but it is the shock and the evolution of the demoralisation that seems to be the real focus; as he founders 'Through craters, corpses,/Stumps of horses, guns and trees' he asks:

> What are the rules for the solitary
> Soldier?

Of course, there are none, because

> ... No one
> Had drilled enterprise into us.

And so 'I ran', and joined those

> Who had hobbled their way back, stubbornly,
> Without heroism.

And 'hobbled' he remains, through Part 2, whose sub-title "SPOILS OF PEACE" is double edged:

> ... I latched on to my red-edged learning,

> Investing sensibly in job, house, car,
> Wife and children, dog and skivvy,

becoming a salesman (and commenting, in explanation: 'In a world fit for heroes, heroism/Is *de trop* ...'). So, he says, '[I] Sold my soul to keep myself safe', incapable of relating in any significant human way to the family he acquires, except in the way of a soldier schooled to trust nobody and nothing, not even his wife (the short parenthetical interpolation here recalls the day of battle recorded in Part 1: the effect of that day's losses, in other words, continues to blight), and can only speak in the dehumanised language of that world:

> ... somehow I had enlisted
> A saboteur, not a friend (my friend
> Died). She gave me nothing

To complain of; collaborated in all
Transactions, ...

Towards the end of the poem, again recalling an expression from Part 1
describing his flight and its psychological causes,

I could do only what I did,
What the primitive man I muzzle
Inside me made me do ...),

he confesses:

My primitive man is dead, crushed
By cordial years of cronies. I couldn't
Speak straight now if I tried.

Ironically, in a way he does, sufficiently to tell his tale of diminished
survival. In what ways has the self-sufficient, emotionally moribund, self-
styled 'tin soldier', the perennial survivor from Hans Andersen's story,
been — that final, ambivalent word — 'constant'? I have suggested the
narrative drift of the poem rather than examined it in the detail its length
seems to call for; this long, parabolic monologue is unique in the poet's
output to date, and its significance seems to reach out beyond the confines
of a volume whose final poem, "Standing To", seems a more appropriate
summation.

Voices Off (1984)

A mere two years after the lengthy *Standing To* came this new,
sizeable volume. In the Interview, UAF draws attention to her awareness
of three new strands in the writing, and this is borne out by the contents:
the condition of women (e.g."From the Third Storey"); France (e.g.
"Cluny: Five Senses, Two Beasts and a Lady"); and S. Martin's College (e.g.
most of the sub-section *MILES TO GO*). But it is not so easy to categorise
the entire contents. The volume is again peopled almost entirely by *people*
of various sorts and conditions exhibiting a spectrum of authorial attitudes
ranging from admiration ("Robert Lindsay's Hamlet", "Tony/Fabian
OSB"), through edgy amusement ("'Soothing and Awful'") to contempt
(not much of this, as one might expect, but the second part of "Patients" is
the most contemptuous of the "hospital" poems, of which it is the sole
representative in this volume). Again, I have to comment on the thematic
ingenuity of several poems: "Growing Up", "Cluny ...", "From the Third
Storey", "Seminar: Felicity and Mr Frost". In this section, I shall focus on
two of these (they are the most effective as well as the most original in the
volume, I think) and on the rest of the "S. Martin's" group, including
"Seminar: Felicity and Mr Frost"; and finally, on what I arbitrarily but not

without demonstrable reason, consider to be several further important poems in the volume. (The poet says in the Interview that she's not sure which are her "best" poems, but with limited space I have to cut corners and make decision; and will comment on "Northmen", "The Person from Porlock", and "Local Poet".) As a brief post-script, as we are at the limit of what was available to the Penguin *Selected Poems*, I shall try to discover what principles underpin the particulars of the volume: by then there ought to be little need to labour the points.

The disarmingly dead-pan title "Cluny: Five Senses, Two Beasts and a Lady" heads one of the most engaging and original poems in the volume, full of verbal fun and in design as intricate as the tapestry that inspired it and almost controls it until, in the final verse, we briefly 'Amble' into Alice in Wonderland territory as the speaker recalls it. Again, it will make for more tedious reading than I intend if I try to draw a map of the poem. There are intertwining strands: the speaker contemplates and interprets the Cluny tapestry *The Lady and the Unicorn*, a tempting detail from which decorates the book's cover, sometimes with a saucy ambiguity which puts a gloss on the details which the tapestry maker seems, from the detail we are offered on the cover, scarcely to have intended:

> With eight fingers and two thumbs the lady
> Handles her portable organ...
>
> Unicorn is having his horn stroked
> By the lady. He is thrilled to bits;

'Lindis', it appears in v. 7 has been the guide 'through the tapestry', as indeed through the city and its ways, but perhaps the heavy-handed teacher, who appears in v. 6 and who 'rubs in the moral' offered by the tapestry's details, is also parodied elsewhere. Sometimes the details of the tapestry are brought to vivid, sometimes comic, life, and threading the poem are one-off shots of contemporary Paris with its 'aromatic shop girls' and 'aseptic Métro'. Each of the first five verses focuses on one sense, formally declared — '*La Voie*', '*Le Toucher*', and so on — and looks at different parts of the tapestry in turn, with its several different representations of each of the characters (Lady, Unicorn, Lion, and various other attendant animals) doing different things until, in v. 6, Lion and Unicorn 'Have reverted to heraldry'. The total effect is a kaleidoscope of sensuous and busy activity in which details from the tapestry are juxtaposed with the real-life details. (There would be a more pedantic way of putting this if one recalls the penetration of the present by the past in so many poems.) As I warned, a tedious comment on what is a poem with wit, liveliness and charm, and readily apprehensible, as my sample shows:

Unicorn eyes his head
In the lady's mirror. His tail has turned
Perpendicular with excitement as her hand lies
Human on his withers. Two cloven feet
Rest on her lap. This is for Lindis,
Who led me among the astute French faces,
Highbrow graffiti, imperial strut of trees
Corks in the well-rinsed gutters, painted
Pools of Giverny. Lion looks out
Of his century at us. You can see his tongue.
He is trying not to snigger. *La Voie.*

The second of the thematically-ingenious poems I shall comment on is "From the Third Storey": the reference in the title is to *Jane Eyre*'s mad Mrs. Rochester, who in the poem is finally set free 'to tell/Truth of mistress, divorcée, mother', and so on, in fact of all the various women writers whose problem lives are sketched in the poem; the mad noises off from the Third Storey (pun here: they *are* all novelists!) which punctuate the sketches ironically function as the writers' never-articulated complaints, and they become progressively vocal and insistent, from the early 'a curious/Laugh' to 'shouting out/Till they could hear her a mile off.' If one said po-facedly that the poem is about the unrecognised and unspoken difficulties that have beset women writers from Jane Austen to Jean Rhys (through, chronologically in the poem, Charlotte Brontë, Mrs. Gaskell, George Eliot and Virginia Woolf; none of them named, deliberately left anonymous, as their problems are invisible too), it wouldn't be wrong, but it wouldn't be anything like the poem, which wears its thesis wittily and lightly. A sample might give a truer idea of what it's actually like:

Aunt Jane scribbles in the living-room,
When visitors come, she stuffs her work
Under the blotter, and joins in the chat.

(In the third storey, a curious
Laugh; distinct, formal, mirthless.)

Daughter Charlotte's first care is to discharge
Her household and filial duties. Only then
May she admit herself to her own bright sphere.

(There were days when she was quite silent;)

'Aunt Jane' is what she is to the world, 'scribbles' is its estimate of what she does, 'stuffs' is appropriate for how the world would regard what she's writing/how she has to hide it, 'chat' is the LCM of trivial exchange — and so on: that is, the words are casually exact. All the women are in effect one ('*I have called myself so many/Different names*') and the poem ends darkly with another ironic quotation from Jean Rhys, '*Now at last I know/Why I was brought here/And what I have to do*'. Writing about women is not all that *A Watching Brief* is concerned with, but it is a part.

The "S. Martin's" group was largely reprinted in Peng. (you will miss there a delightful satire, "Seminar: Life; Early Poems", on the note-taking ineptitude of 'Red-hair' who 'heads her page: *H.B. Yeats* [confusing him with the thing she's writing with, perhaps], who was '*proud of his ancestory*'). Like the "hospital" poems scattered through the volumes, the "college" poems are varied and no two cover the same ground. The expected sharp eye is at work in "The First Years Arrive" and "Being a Student"; there is a laconic monologue spoken by a cleaner, quoted in Ch. One, and a wicked satire on pedantry headed by an (unintentionally) comic quotation from Professor Terry Eagleton, "Knowing about Sonnets"; and one of the volume's most attractive offerings, "Seminar: Felicity and Mr Frost". Here, a seminar is being run (at least, that is the idea) on two poems by Robert Frost, evidently "Mending Wall" and "Stopping by Woods on a Snowy Evening". 'Marigold-headed Felicity (three)', brought along to the seminar by her mother 'because of a hole in the roof', is the poem's chief living character (UAF is invariably good at children, treats them with sharp-eyed, unsentimental understanding). This is yet another poem whose inner workings are hard to summarise but which readily communicates. For instance:

> ... Mr Frost has brought a wall
>
> With holes in it. The holes grow
> Larger and larger as the sun
> Walks round the room. Felicity
> Opens her mouth in a yawn like a hole.
>
> *I didn't understand the story*
> *The man was telling us* she says clearly
> Underneath the table ...
>
> Mr Frost is preoccupied. He
> Has promises to keep. And miles to go.

Here, the speaker recreates what reads like Felicity's gloss on the Frost poem (Felicity's thoughts being coloured by the domestic hole in the roof, and later obligingly and amusingly exemplified in the simile of her yawn); Felicity, bored by the whole thing, entertains/disrupts the seminar by her out-loud, child-honest comment; and "Mr. Frost's" actual poem surfaces, as it does elsewhere in the poem, through the watchful ear of the observer/speaker (the complete four-line stanza quoted here keeps the hole business going in a vivid metaphor from the child's world). One of the poet's most winning pieces, I have to say.

I shall focus on just three more of the poems in this volume which I find of particular interest: "Northmen", "Local Poet", and the one which by careful planning follows this, "The Person's Tale". "Northmen", as I said in Ch. One, takes a more positive view than is usual regarding this subject, particularly in the final section, because it takes a more than usually long view. The first section deals with the 'Northmen's' activities to the point where they 'dug in' at Durham; the second with their relics; the third, in which they are referred to for the first times as 'Vikings', their more common, plunder-saturated name having presumably been witheld until the case had been made on their behalf, with their legacy and achievement — which is, paradoxically, to disappear,

> ... leaving their Viking selves
> Underground,

and to become settlers who leave relics both grim and artistic of how they were

> For ploughmen to stumble on after.

In effect, the poem is circular, for its temporal ending is no ending but implicit continuity. What is notable in the poem is what I have again to call its sharp particularity, in whose language implicit understanding for the energy and culture of its subject makes the poem a kind of celebration: an alternative view, though even within the poem they are still, as their relics remind us, fearsome in their forcefulness:

> Their relics are savage, momentous:
> A sword ritually disfigured,
> Then buried, like a man, at Gotland ...
>
> The sea chanted inside the gaunt swords,
> Two-edged slashers of embedded waves ...

The final section, from which I quoted in Ch. One, is neither lament nor anti-climax, and its valedictory last lines, reminiscent of Ted Hughes' "Thistles",

> Only a few Norse names are standing
> Still, like thistles, among the furrows ...

do not annul what has preceded them. The poem, like others in the collection, (e.g. "Tomorrow and", "Robert Lindsay's Hamlet") is in syllabic verse (here of nine syllables per line), and this confers an appropriately-rough formality.

Finally, the two poems about poets, "Local Poet", an anonymous Gloucestershire poet with very limited talent, and "The Person's Tale", an alternative view of the famous Coleridge explanation of how his vision, which was to have been re-created in a comprehensive "Kubla Khan", was interrupted by "a person from Porlock". In this version, the interrupter is no 'person' but a "parson", and himself a poet: thus, in these two juxtaposed poems, in each case one poet comments on another, in the case of the first with an understanding which amounts to wry sympathy, in the case of the second with pompous denigration (if, as we know from biographical sources, not without some unsavoury truth, as Coleridge detains the 'person' at his door

> With chronicles of colic, stomach, bowels,
> Of nightly sweats, the nightmare, cramps, diarrhoea ...)

"Local Poet" once again exhibits some sympathetic understanding without pulling punches: he *is* (we believe) an awful poet and is wholly unaware of this, or of the speaker's true estimate of his worth as a writer, and that he has put her on a spot by asking her to select some of his poems for a competition. She does her best:

> We settle which to send. He's disappointed
>
> By what I like, I know he has no chance
> Of winning. Does he trust me? No, I think ...
>
> I hope he won't read this.

Earlier in the poem, we have some "proper" poetry, but not by this 'poet/For wild things' which he has become, but by the speaker writing for him, as it were:

> ... [he] tells how blackbirds
>
> Lob home through ivy ...
>
> Long dead shires with hooves
>
> As big as buckets ...
>
> ... bees feverish
> For marrow pollen ...

The tone of the poem, like so many in these collections, moves and fluctuates between some degree of satire and some degree of sympathy, and the blend reads like unvarnished truth:

> ... most of all
>
> I like his garden ones, about the flowers
> He grows but cannot spell ...

His mistrust of the competition judge is ill-founded and faithfully reported:

> '... *This judge —*
> *Where's he from anyway? He won't know here.*'

"The Person's Tale", with its parodic Chaucer title, is *all* "faithfully reported", being a dramatic monologue spoken by the self-important parson himself in self-justification: a piece of highly-entertaining pastiche of period idiom:

> That the Muses have no more fervent
> Devotee than myself may not be generally
> Known outside Porlock ...

The appearance of Coleridge, reportedly stoned out of his mind and stinking (the refined '*person*' is far too nice to say so in those terms — 'neglected hygiene/Rendering contiguity less than welcome') is a characteristic piece of irreverence: and indeed the poem is one of the book's funniest.

I promised to attempt a summary of what seem to be these poems' implicit guiding positives (and those of preceding volumes too, no doubt, would confirm them): stoicism, honesty, coping, doing what has to be done, trying to *understand* and to have sympathy where it's called for; carrying on ("Tomorrow and", "Visiting Mr Lewis", "Tyneside in December"); and doing it well, achieving to the best of one's ability and with integrity ("Robert Lindsay's Hamlet", "Northmen", even, in his way, "Local Poet"). — An unimpressive and reductive set of abstractions of the sort that UAF mercifully avoids.

A Watching Brief (1987).

Three years on from *Voices Off* came another substantial volume. By now, there are obvious indications of impressive arrival on the poetry scene: commissions from the BBC. and the Cheltenham Festival, an award from the Society of Authors of a Travelling Scholarship, an Arts Council Fellowship at S. Martin's College, inclusion in the Poetry Book Society Supplement three years running. There are in this volume *some* different emphases, e.g. only one "hospital" poem (these are to return in some quantity in the next volume, *Neck-Verse*), fewer poems concerned with "tradition" (but still some significant references), more personal and anecdotal poems; and a considerable and explicit emphasis on "watching" and observing, not merely where it might be expected, as in the case of the doctor in "The Doctor" or the painter in "La Débâcle ...", but also in more personal poems such as "In Residence" and "Confessio Amantis", and even in the unlikely "Halley's Comet 1985-6". All in all, the volume presents a not unfamiliar variety of concerns and a familiar variety of styles, from 'terse and cogent' to diffuse and demotic, and frequently exhibiting that Alan Bennett-like capacity for catching the nuances of "ordinary" speech. The tone continues to walk the tightrope between the serious (never the solemn) and the frivolous or purely funny (and, as such, almost defies analysis as much as it calls for quotation). Again, the personal poems are neither embarrassingly self-indulgent nor an excuse for self-exhibition or breast-beating, or any of the other disagreeable things readers of contemporary poetry at large are fairly used to; and such poems are peopled with round, credible characters, often family members but conceived in novelist's terms. For some readers, the interest of personal poems will no doubt be that they "throw light on" the poet, and perhaps they will thus be more "enlightened" by such poems than by others; this particular reader prefers to regard them as poems, not as grist for the biog-critical mill. The significance is in people in contexts.

What else we have here from the point of view of category is, firstly, a group of dramatic monologues with the customary range of speakers, in this case from Halley's Comet itself and an adolescent writing to his/her hero, Laurie Lee (one of the most appealing poems), to Mary of the Mary/Martha/Jesus story in the New Testament. I have also to say at some point, and will do so here, that what printed comment has come my way has tended to play down the elements of fun, snook-cocking, sauciness, laughter and sendings-up of all degrees. Such things are, of course, the very devil to anatomise — nothing goes colder on criticism than such a range of "entertainment". Frequently in the course of this poetry, you are likely to be asked, in the middle of what you had assumed to be a piece of such jauntiness, to adjust your response and face in another direction: a case in point occurs in "Confessio Amantis" (which for a start is scarcely a "confessio amantis" pure and simple): watch the way the poem without warning goes into anti-climactic self-satire:

> ... I am also
> Watchman, who waketh, generally without a clue
> Of what he waketh for ...

Secondly, we have more college-based or -inspired poems; and some overt concern with women's points of view, feminist poems in the generic sense but without the shrillness or political drum-banging which have occasionally been features of feminist poetry in the Western world; once again, the variety of approach and technical devices are to be registered. One poem of the genre which must be commented on in some detail, considered sufficiently important to warrant an entire page of supporting or explanatory notes, is "Three Women Wordsworths". Another poem to be taken seriously is the utterly different "Unauthorised Version" with its Liverpudlian-seeming speaker — one of those disarming mixtures of the funny and serious I referred to earlier. (Readers will find their own more precise terms to displace "funny" and "serious" as they seem to be called for by different poems: "variety" is again the obvious word to use). Further poems concerning women are "Bronwen" a sensitive Aussie toughie, so to speak; and "Of Mutability", in which we are presented with a character, perhaps the 'Meg' of the dedication*, who, like the house she lives in, has a "knack of enduring". The poem has the following lines which, as well as instancing the poet's fondness for lists and catalogues of relevant items, emphasise a positive implicit in much of the poetry throughout:

> ... things done,
> Meals cooked, fires lit, trees planted, words said,
> Poems observed, have their own posterity ...

Fruitful, unspectacular, enjoined (not merely "dutiful") activity; and poetry, 'observed', note, takes its place in the roll call of the celebration of such modestly honourable, abiding ('posterity') matters.

One or two further generalisations should be made before I comment on a few particularly notable poems, as before personally but not arbitrarily selected. (The problem, from this point of view alone, is always to select from a range of interesting writing: none of these volumes — as has been known to happen in the poetry world — is draped round a single or a few "outstanding" poems, and I simply cannot comment on all the worthwhile candidates in the detail I should like, and have to scatter what wider references I can amongst my generalising and categorising, as above.) The volume is permeated with "controlled", that is, unelaborated and emotionally reined-in, references to "love" and "home"; and to the humble, the unlovely and the ordinary. (But, as I've said, UAF, like Alan Bennett, picks up and contextualises what may in itself be "ordinary" but which is

---

* The precision of my counting is not wholly reliable, but I have counted 32 separate personal dedications in the various volumes' poems, apart from the many poems directly addressed to individual people where no specific dedication is needed. Apart from the biographical implications, which are not my concern, one thing confirmed by such a profusion of dedications, if one needed it, is surely the paramount interest in other people and their activities which such a generous habit exemplifies. Perhaps it is also rather obvious that all these dedicatees, according to the contents of their poems, seem to exemplify in their active lives the purposeful, modest, necessary ways of being, often in spite of personal difficulty or distress, that are some of the poems' consistent positives.

elevated to the status of the noteworthy or the hilarious, or even the wise.) There are references to the concept of "exile", often used in "away from home" situations; more references to soldiers and the military; and everywhere *people*, in particular and precisely-drawn places and contexts.

Having made a general survey of the volume with a few sneaked-in references to particular poems, I shall now focus on three of the prime contenders for more detailed comment: "Three Women Wordsworths", "Dear Mr Lee", and "Looking for Jorvik": in a nutshell sort of way, they illustrate the variety of tone and texture which continue to be dominant features of the poetry.

"Three Women Wordsworths" is perhaps the most obviously "important" poem in the book, and the poet has been at some pains (too many?) to ensure we have all the background information we need so as not to misunderstand the poem. (Whether poems should need notes at all, and if so what kind, is still a live issue*.) The notes' opening sentence: 'These three poems are perhaps a gloss of Coleridge's remark about Wordsworth: "living wholly among *Devotees* — having every the minutest Thing, almost his very Eating and Drinking, done for him by his Sister, or Wife."'. Sour grapes by the bunch there, surely; but evidently the poem (I shall regard it as a single poem with three parts: they do reflect on each other) is to be a put-down of Wordsworth the man ('dear Idiot Man' Mary, his wife, calls him in her part of the poem) and a deploring of the subordinate roles for which wife and sister are cast by the Sublime Egotist (and Egoist). Certainly "the facts" and their gloss speak for themselves. Of "Daffodils":

> Years later William knocked it together;
> Mary gave her two lines†. But it was Dorothy
> Did the fieldwork ...

as indeed *she* did; what results is a poem 'The National trust can use', but Dorothy's journal entry has a 'straggle of unplanned delights and scrambles' which 'defy the taming mind' of William (which missed such things as '*N.B. Deer /In Gowbarrow Park like skeletons*': was this such a loss, do we think?). This is a crude summary of the substance of the first part of the poem, DEER IN GOWBARROW PARK, but it takes no account of the nice irories in opening:

---

* I have throughout mentioned sources which are unacknowledged but which I have identified: the issue of "notes or no notes" has been around since, say, "Absalom and Achitophel" and I have no space to argue it out with reference to *these* poems — in general, I believe knowing sources here to enhance, not determine, value or meaning, and that there is no deliberate obfuscation, ever.

† She did: 'They flash ... solitude'

> Not a gallant old warhorse of a poem,
> Scarred from the student wars, but an indomitable
> Little hackney, docile with twelve-year-olds ...

Surely, in spite of 'indomitable' (which is less elevated in the scheme of things than 'gallant'), rather a put-down: the resonance of 'hackney' will not be missed, nor will the relegation of the poem to suitability for twelve-year-olds, 'Who may not understand *inner eyes* and/*Tranquil recollecting*, but know a *King Alfred*/When they see one, and can imagine lots'. The misquoting is, of course, part of the put-down. The second part focuses on the continued ignoring of Dorothy in the equation, the organising of the house for his express personal comfort and poet's ease, and the time-consuming pampering. (The Rug "says" that it was 'Spun, dyed and knitted for the Poet's knees'. Somehow poets ought not to have anything as ordinary as 'knees', not Wordsworth anyhow.) Then there's the sheepfold (which led to the writing of "Michael") seen by William and Dorothy, the aspect of which is recorded with wicked irony (UAF's not Dorothy's) in the Journal:

> *Built nearly in the form of a heart*
> *Unequally divided.*

Many hints to be taken here. Finally there is wife Mary's poem: there is her self-effacement, more of Dorothy as she became an 'incontinent and senile baby,/Farted and belched, shrieked, sang and swore and spat' — this is *her* final portion. Mary's is to 'nurse into print' and name 'the Work' (i.e. "The Prelude") just as she had nursed her 'dear Idiot Man,/With his bad nights, his love child' and all the rest; and the poem finally becomes plainly denigratory:

> [He] never noticed things till Dorothy wrote them

> Into his journal; was put right by eight-year-olds*:
> Couldn't take it in, the leech gatherer's message, missed
> The crowning moment when they crossed the Alps ...

and so on. All true, of course. All relevant to the poetry? And how does this accord with the comment on Wordsworth in the Interview? There the silent debate must begin: but, of course, this poem is not simply biography, it does not simply deal in "facts": it is a fine, subtle, witty, serious, finally touching and sad poem, as Mary offers thanks to the Almighty

*He was, in "We Are Seven"

> ... after eight hard years of marriage
> For *the first letter of love that has been*
>
> *Exclusively my own.*

Big deal, one cannot help remarking; but one also registers her phrase 'dear Idiot Man'.

"Dear Mr Lee" is, in contrast, almost sheerly delightful (I say "almost" because one of its characters is a 'Mr Smart'): a character study of an adolescent who isn't terribly bright perhaps, but loves *Cider with Rosie* well but not sufficiently wisely for examination purposes and for her/his ironical (par for the course in this) English teacher, the ambiguously-named 'Mr Smart', who urges her or him to be 'terse and cogent' (a phrase, it may be noticed, that I have from time to time hi-jacked for my own different purposes); but confesses, 'I'm not much good at terse and cogent'. So, s/he says to 'Dear Laurie'

> I didn't want to write a character-sketch
> of your mother under headings, it seemed
> wrong somehow when you'd made her so lovely,
> and I didn't much like those questions
> about *social welfare in the rural community*
> and *the seasons as perceived by an adolescent* ...

All of us in the trade have set such questions, as UAF well knows (and may have once set!). The poem was commissioned by the Cheltenham Festival of Literature for a programme celebrating the life and work of Laurie Lee, and one trusts he enjoyed it. (It is also, I have po-facedly to add, in this respect a disciple, if not the actual teacher, of the unknown original 'Mr Smart', a poem about integrity and priorities.)

"Looking for Jorvik" (cf. "Northmen" in *Voices Off*) is also somewhat annotated: with an explanation about how Egil saved his neck by composing a Head-Ransom song in praise of Eric Bloodaxe who would have had him put to death had he not done so: a classic instance of what Dr Johnson had in mind about threat of such a thing concentrating the mind wonderfully. More on this subject when we reach *Neck-Verse*: but we should register the poem's incidental, and UAF's characteristic, testimony to the power of poetry. In the event, the poem is a piece of narrative depicting the 'time capsule' experience which contemporary Yorkies and their visitors are having in York, transported into the Viking past of 'Jorvik', i.e. York, by a dark journey those who have had it will not need to read about and those who haven't would need too long a rigmarole to describe. But the poem, in an obvious sort of way, is about the surfacing of the Viking past in a physical, and symbolic, way in the contemporary world:

> ... through the one
> Date everybody knows*, to the ancestral
>
> Mutter and reek. This is then, now. We are
> Where it was, it is ...

The 'Jorvik' experience is, in spite of — no, surely in part because of — the trivial comments of Alan Bennett-type characters (*'That wouldn't/Interest me. But for someone like Barbara,/Who's a real intellectual ...'*) which jostle with remarks of deadly earnest (*'I dabbled my blade in/Bloodaxe's boy'*), a perfect example of how the past penetrates the present; and the poem hasn't finished on this subject, for the speaker has 'unearthed my own past under Jorvik's shaft' by 'thinking suddenly':

> *I am on my way to life*

because "on my way to you": and the poem finally hints of love. Thus via saving your neck by writing, words as salvation , we come to the final volume to date:

Neck-Verse (1992).

We have come a fair if not excessively long way in time terms since *Side Effects* of 1978, and it is not surprising that most of the poems in the first four books are variations on themes early established. (And, as I have stressed, there is considerable variety of all kinds and in all ways throughout.) This latest volume too has its quota of "personal" poems — poems written in the 1st person singular or family poems including several thematically-significant ones. I have written already of "Descent" with its blank, bleak, restrained, and finally stoical positives. In another poem, "Familiars", a similar image occurs:

> I submit to darkness

ends the first verse. This is a poem avowedly looking for what at one point it calls 'the way out': but it does not find one. There are also a number of "hospital" poems again; also some portraits, including some of the young, invariably done with insight and understanding, and also of the old; and there are a few dramatic monologues. There are traces of love poetry, scarcely complete love poems, everywhere. The short "Idyll" most nearly encapsulates the sustaining domestic positive in this and indeed previous books, to which the "idyllic" condition described in the poem aspires; the condition of

*1066

Maybe heaven. Or maybe
We can get so far in this world. I'll believe we can.

The final two sentences are interestingly ambiguous: what is 'so far': as far as heaven? Or "so far and no farther"? Does this not suggest a degree of caution in a world which is, after all, still 'this world' and not 'heaven'? And we notice also 'I'll believe', which is subtly different from the categorical "I believe". I trust the travellers in the twittering twilit world of the London Underground who are currently gazing at a poster version of this poem are mindful of such niceties.

But, as well as these familiar directions and indirections, there are new ones, as there usually are: a new kind of hinting (in most instances no more) of personal suffering or difficulty; significantly, as I have said, in "Descent"; also present in "A Life", which has an extended conceit of life in terms of a prison sentence. I find several poems, including the obviously important "Word Games", unusually difficult: not merely complex, which any reader of Fanthorpe's poetry will have come to expect, but cryptic, with strange logical connections, poems in which the meaning seems to be in hiding; in at least two, "Doubles" and "Familiars", there is some kind of truth-searching, the nature of which is not entirely clear (though *some* of "Familiars" is clear enough). My voyage of discovery in *Neck-Verse*, which came out as recently as 1992, is thus more than usually incomplete and some of my conclusions more than usually inconclusive.

The poet puts on record in the Interview her awareness of the interest in words as such in the volume. "Word Games" is obviously and explicitly about language and its range of functions, from entertainment to life-saving (but then this has been implicit in the poetry from the start). In the first part, COMFORTABLE WORDS, there is an exemplification of the capacity of words to divert, on the one hand, as in the case of the linguistic entertainment value of crossword puzzles (where 'Friday, of course, is a man,/And a duck means nothing'), and on the other hand to fail to encapsulate or relieve the suffering of the speaker or express that of her dying child:

> ... There can be nothing
> Worse than this, and this is now ...

> ... My baby's local language
> Is anguish. Shrieks are all she says

In the second part, NECK-VERSE, the speaker (another) cites 'A cat's cradle of country proverbs' which, to the extent that they are 'reassuring halloos from the past' (the link with the "tradition" theme is evident) are helpful embodiments of folk wisdom, 'To take the ache out of Age' (the speaker feels both these entities) 'to comfort me'. The most serious and extreme power of words to solve problems is the 'Neck-Verse' referred to in the footnote; the capacity to read the first verse of Psalm 51 was once taken to prove that the reader had been ordained and so was exempted from murder trial in a secular court. (In fact, this ultimate capacity of the saving power of words is not so closely exemplified in this poem as it is, at a secular level, in "Looking for Jorvik" in WB — q.v. my remarks in Ch. One). Perhaps, I thought as I read and re-read the poem, this is the kind of seminal poem which in a sense sums up past preoccupations and might be a concept-hoard, if not a word-hoard, for others: the subject is perhaps too important to the poet for this to be the last word on the subject: as the next poems declares, 'Words are my element' ("Awkward Subject").

The majority of the poems are as "approachable" as usual, and it is on some of the hypothetical best ones I shall now concentrate; and as usual there are too many candidates for selection for this book's small space. So I shall focus on "Elegy for a Cat", for its humour and its seriousness: "Neighbours", as some kind of ultimate in dramatic monologues; "The Poet's Companion" for its sheer inventiveness (though I would much prefer to read it entire and aloud); and finally, and perhaps appropriately, a serio-comic portrait of another medical misfit, "Superannuated Psychiatrist".

"Elegy for a Cat" is from the beginning not merely another commemorative poem (though it is everywhere that too):

> Yours was the needlework, precise and painful
> As claws on a loved naked shoulder, that sewed us
> Back into that Merthyr morning

The typical conceit (needlework/claws/sewed) of these lines suggests that the cat (never named, too significant perhaps to be so limited to familiarity or particularity) has a difficult role to play in establishing a new relationship ('our outlandish outfit', amongst 'Invisible agog neighbours' with problems barely hinted here; a role which, against the grain of its nature ('severed .../From your own earth') it continued to play:

> Exiled in Gloucestershire, you domesticated
> It for us ...
>
> ... you chose us to be
> Your territory.

I would not expect a non-lover of cats to appreciate how delicately the poem manages to thread a course between the Scylla of sentimentality and the Charybdis of unlikely anthropomorphism, but it does: though this cat has insights (as they do):

> You who saw love, where innocent others
> Saw only convenience.

But it is still and abidingly cat, and as individual and idiosyncratic as they all are: it is described with both wit and with rare affection:

>   ... elbowing your way
> Up bodies like a midshipman up rigging,
> Your whiskers wet with passion, sitting with one ear
> In a human mouth, to keep warm.

The cat's reciprocated love for the speaker, more warmly, less restrainedly expressed than usual, is an expression (in the poem) of that of its joint guardians for each other: it is missed and mourned both for itself and because of the role it played, however unwittingly:

> Haunt us still, dear first-footer,
> First to live with us, first to confirm
> Us as livers-together ...

Small wonder that

>   ... You are there quite often,
> Dear tabby blur, in my bad eye's corner.

Even for an unusually sensitive poet, an unusually sensitive poem: if I had to choose one from the entire *opera*, this would possibly be the one.

    The primary joke of "Neighbours" is that we don't know, and are never informed, who the speakers are: but birds of some kind and in some quantity; and the 'neighbours', apart from the humans who get a final footnote mention, are other birds. The fun throughout derives from anthropomorphism: all the birds behave like well-defined human types and are described in human-type images. The poem, thus, is in a long tradition of such writing, going back at least as far as "The Owl and the Nightingale"; the 'Collared couple' (i.e. pigeons) who 'lived at number one,/In the guttering' (if you miss the point of identification in 'Collared', you have some leg-pulled way to go before the next clue) 'might have been R.C.' because of 'the missus's ... tender ... slightly Madonna-ish' nape and psalm-like three-note chant. 'The Blackies', on the other hand, 'were a racketty lot' who

>   ... zoomed home like motorbikes revving.

So the fun of birds-as-humans continues until we reach 'Two terrorists': unseen, as terrorists are, but

> They talk of her yellow eyes, her butcher's poise,
> The pigeon bleeding in her taloned fist.

and suddenly the poem has gone savage on you: note the sustained anthropomorphic language — 'fist' — which, with its adjective, puts a new construction on savagery of the human kind.

"The Poet's Companion" somehow keeps going by endless invention: we know it is written by a poet, so we are expecting some kind of autobiographical splurge: what we get is, in effect, a satire on the legendary demandingness of poets, expressed in a dead-pan, reasonable-seeming, almost guide-to-the-subject catalogue of essential attributes that the "poet's companion" has to have; but the fun has *some* (undefined) underlying degree of "I do mean this", and the catalogue of attributes never becomes either surreal or wholly unreasonable (except in a cumulative way). So the ideal "poet's companion" *would* desirably have all these skills and attributes as far as 'The Poet' is concerned. But the double-takes of satire have more up their sleeves: this *is* all written by a poet, called U.A. Fanthorpe, and to that extent the dreamed-up aggregation of attributes is also a piece of self-satire implying, perhaps, "I'm like this, too". It all sounds in such leaden prose so heavy and complicated, and the poem is so light and entertaining, and funny — all qualities easier illustrated than anatomised:

> Should keep a good address book. In public will lead
> The laughter, applause, the unbearably moving silence.
> Must sustain with grace
>
> The role of Muse, with even more grace the existence
> Of another eight or so, also camera's curious peeping
> When the Poet is reading a particularly
>
> Randy poem about her, or (worse) about someone else.

The skill that went into the making of this is well concealed, unobtrusive: it's there in the line-breaks with their subsequent surprises ('will lead/The laughter,' 'particularly/Randy poem'), in the (self-)satirically precious 'unbearably', the throwaway 'or so' (there are precisely nine). Part of the fun (and all the other related things) is the way 'The Poet' (always self-important upper-case) can keep going for thirteen three-line stanzas of "demands"; and the final, *barbed*, joke is the relevation that this poet, after all, and how characteristic of the MCPs, is a male:

> Must be ... well able ...

[To] sustain with undiminished poise
That saddest dedication: *lastly my wife,*

Who did the typing.

Quite finally, "Superannuated Psychiatrist": not wholly another of the *bêtes-noires* of the genre "Doctor" but an unconscious provider of entertainment and a scapegoat, and so, especially compared with his high-flying successor ('Smelling of aftershave and ambition'), he is a (shall we say) not wholly unsympathetic figure. The tone is pitched between contempt and amusement, and once again it is the inventiveness of the detail that is telling:

> Old scallywag scapegoat has skedaddled,
> Retired at last to bridge and both kinds of bird-watching ...

> How we shall miss his reliable shiftiness ...

>   ... Dear foxy quack,
> I relished your idleness, your improvisations,
> Your faith in my powers of you-preservation.
> Who will shoulder our errors now?

It is also in the light of the 'haggis-shaped' doctor in another portrait, "Dear Sir", who is in that poem accused of such crimes as

> ... inconspicuous valour on behalf of underdogs;
> Of exploring humanity's dark places
> And not letting on ...

that 'Old scallywag' stands accused of dereliction of duty as well as having high entertainment value; and thus UAF's declared ambition in the Interview to write a book in which all the parts comment on each other is, in part, and perhaps inevitably, already realised; not for the first time.

In that Interview, I asked U.A. Fanthorpe to speculate about her future plans as a writer and, rather non-committally, she complied. I think it is safe to predict that, whatever direction the poetry may take as the chess piece is moved around (though I am sure it will not be moved to where it does not really wish to be), it will continue to manifest itself in wit, liveliness, sanity, wholesomeness, balance, good sense, and great good humour.

September, 1993.

SLOW LEARNER

U.A.Fanthorpe

It is characteristic of the slow learner not only to learn slowly but also to take a long time to discover that something has in fact been learned. The slow learner is bad at learning, at accepting with grace the status of pupil. I was suspicious of anything my teachers offered me because somehow I had it in my head that the only valuable things to learn were the ones that I could discover for myself.

It was always my ambition to be a writer. However I made this ambition hard to achieve by two basic assumptions, first that my own age-group was homogenous and automatically uninteresting, and second that experience, which is what makes people interesting, is the result of age. These were quite reasonable assumptions to make in the nineteen-fifties, before to be a teenager meant automatically to have status. My contemporaries and I slank through life, camouflaged to look like our parents, waiting till we were thirty, when by some magic process we should become independent and astute. At university, one's callowness was even more evident since many ex-servicemen and women were around, finishing off degrees that war had interrupted, and redolent with Experience. Naturally, such students were far more interesting to the tutors than my generation could ever be.

In default of a war, it seemed neccessary to invent some other form of baptism by fire. This was given me, but being a slow learner, of course I failed to recognise it. As a result of an accident I had to spend three months on my back in the gynae-and-orthopaedic ward of the Radcliffe Infirmary. Here was life enough for anyone to write about; there was Ruby, the ward maid, who was simple; there was Nancy, in the bed opposite mine, who was dying; there was Hazel, whose pelvis had been crushed by a lorry and who could never have any more children (I remember the lorry-driver coming one day to see her; he just leaned over the foot of the bed and said nothing); there was Mrs Dining Room, so called because she was apparently the only person in the ward who had such a thing; there was Mrs Green, the authority on turkeys from Wootton Bassett, and Mrs Jenkins, who hated wasting time and insisted, much to sister's fury, in operating a loom which was erected in and around her bed among the traction apparatus.

I found this closed world so fascinating that it was quite difficult to extract me when I was mobile again. My parents were horrified at my idea that I should swap courses and become a nurse ("after all the money that's been spent on your education"). The University careers department said, reasonably, that all I was really qualified for was teaching, and I wasn't really properly qualified even for that yet. It suddenly became important to raise money, and I pocketed my aims and went off to acquire a teaching diploma — my reason, such as it was, being that since experience equalled people, and schools were full of people, I might be able to get where I wanted to be quickest by this route.

However, I had not realised the seductiveness with which schools handle their apprentices. I entered full of knowledge about the Scottish Chaucerians and the Fight at Finnsberg, which nobody wanted; instead it was indicated that if I behaved myself there was a chance that next year I might be put in charge of the Bicycle Sheds. That first step was followed by the lure of the Junior Library. It was really quite like Spenser's Bower of Bliss, had I realised it. I went on acquiring minor responsibilities and inflating my self-esteem, and the only writing that got done was when I was asked for some bagatelle or other, for an anniversary or a leaving party. Sixteen years later I awoke from academic slumber and realised that sixteen years' growth of pupils had gone on to find experience, live among people and generally done the things that I'd wanted to, while I had contented myself with working to free them.

By a series of manoeuvres I disentangled myself from pupils, the Burnham Scale and the Bicycle Shed mentality. After that came a brief flurry of courses in counselling, times on the dole, working in Bristol as a *temp* at places like Hoover's complaints department and Butler's Chemicals, and in 1974, having found that the way to get a job was to conceal my qualifications, I contrived to be taken on as clerk/receptionist in a small hospital.

The long boredom of slowly discovering who I was and what I could do was over: poetry struck during my first month behind the desk. I think it started because of the anger and frustration I felt. My job involved organising outpatient clinics, and as I watched the outpatients I began more and more to admire their stoicism, their cheerfulness, their patience. I wanted to do something for them and, as the least qualified person in the hospital, all I could do was listen, suggest a visit to the canteen, show where the lavatories were, or assure them that Dr. X couldn't possibly keep them waiting much longer. It still wasn't my own experience, but that somehow ceased to matter. From my receptionist's glass dugout I watched a world I hadn't imagined, of the epileptic, the depressed, the obsessed, the brain-damaged, the violent, the helpless. I read the case-histories written in official medical language, which had its own peculiar effect on me. I also had time to think things out for myself while pursuing routine occupations. And there was the subtle blessing of the Oxford English dictionary upstairs, in all its 12 original volumes. There was also the *blessing* of a brief solitary lunch-hour. Knowing that 40 minutes was all I had prevented me from indulging in too much pencil-sharpening.

In these circumstances poetry happened to me. I was a witness, and what I saw could not be described in prose, since so much of it was a matter of intuitions, and of rebellion against the hospital's officially reasonable outlook. More importantly, if I didn't write about what I saw, nobody would know about it. I went on, of course, to write of other things, but this was the original impetus. A late developer, as will be obvious from my story so far, I often fail to understand what I've written, or have gradually to come to terms with it. I haven't much control over what I write; if asked for a poem, I can with some effort usually manage it, but only by linking it with some current private obsession.

I've been in love with the English language since I first learned to speak, and I enjoy finding out answers. My poems are mostly, in one way or another, an attempt to deal with an area of darkness in my mind. I'm not able to shed light on the darkness, but it seems important to try. When the poems don't work, it is generally because of a bad habit of putting cheap wit before love.

Appendix B: Interview with U.A.Fanthorpe

Note: This interview was conducted by correspondence: I posed questions and received answers, and what follows is a verbatim transcript arranged in proper interview form.

EW: Do you *mind* being asked questions about your poetry? Would you prefer it to make its own way rather than have "middle people" obtruding?

UAF: No, I don't mind answering questions about poetry that's been published, it's fair game. I have no experience of "middle people" so far, but seeing it's you, I'm looking forward to it!

EW: I hope your anticipation is not disappointed by the reality! — It seems you've been writing poetry seriously for less than twenty years. When did you become aware that writing poetry was something you could do (perhaps had to do?), to the extent of risking giving up your post as Head of English at Cheltenham Ladies College to do it?

UAF: I think there are some false assumptions here. I didn't leave Cheltenham to write poetry but for a fresh start*. I left in 1970 and wrote some prose criticism until 1974, when poetry "struck". I'd been writing poetry for about six months before I felt it might be "working", and important to me.

EW: It's an established fact (which I won't at this point bother to document: but probably will elsewhere) that you are a popular poet, certainly one of the most popular amongst serious contenders. Three questions about this, please: have you any thoughts about *why* this is so? And has this popularity (and early success with *Side Effects*) either helped or hindered you as a writer (and if so, how?)? And do you enjoy your popularity — is it, for instance, for the right reasons, does it do you justice?

UAF: I don't feel I *am* a "popular poet". Being one is a very dubious thing — not to be compared with the "popularity" of a novelist or a pop star or a footballer or Pam Ayres! But if I have some "popularity" I suppose it's because my poetry is mostly accessible and touches on a wide variety of human situations. *Side Effects* wasn't really an "early success". What made a big difference was coming third in the Arvon/*Observer* Poetry Competition of '80-'81. None of it has really made any difference to me as a writer — I'm not aware of being "popular" in a day-to-day way, but

---

* Cf. what "U.A.Fanthorpe writes" on the back cover of *Side Effects*: 'Sixteen years (after beginning to teach at Cheltenham) I decided that the day of dedication to the honest penny was over and I became a middle-aged drop-out in order to write'.

sometimes perhaps at readings, and I do feel then that it's for the right reasons, because they're responding to what I'm saying and the poetry is obviously "working".*

EW: Are you at all aware of what motivates you as a writer (or do you prefer not to know)? What 'sin to you unknown dipped you in ink', as Pope put it? And are you aware of having "developed" as a poet (or do you agree with Wilde as quoted by Larkin, 'Only mediocrities develop'?): or is this one for me rather than for you?

UAF: I'm aware of having *different things brought to my attention* — life moves me around, like a chess piece. In *Side Effects* it was the power structure in a hospital, and sort of broken, forgotten things (canals, folksong, and so on). In *Standing To*, this continued, but death and dreams entered too — and the idea of "standing to", which appears in the last poem there. In *Voices Off* I entered the different world of S. Martin's, Lancaster, and of France; and I was just beginning to see things to say about the condition of women. *Watching Brief* has a lot about women and writers and love, and perhaps *Neck-Verse* is about words and word-users. As for "development" in any other way, I just try to modify the way I write to fit what's coming out. Perhaps this *is* one for you! Something else I could say about motivation: I feel the need to rectify, to correct the balance if I feel things are unfair. Also to find the balance, to *strike* the balance (whether this is a sin unknown or the experience of living in a legal household†, I leave you to assess). If I have any objectives, it's to bear witness, to say, "I have seen this, and no one else was there looking at that precise moment"; especially perhaps on behalf of the dispossessed. In order to write I have to concentrate. And concentration is a form of love.

EW: Are you aware of, conscious of, your thematic material, e.g. a preoccupation with the truth under the appearance, the effective contemporaneity of past and present, the penetration of the serious by the funny, and vice-versa, and that "deep down things" are ultimately worthwhile?

UAF: What's important to me is *people* — even landscapes are important because of what people have done to them and so on. I'm particularly involved with people *who have no voice*: the dead, the dispossessed, or the inarticulate in various ways. I'm not carrying on a "campaign" on their

---

* It is obviously dificult to acquire figures, but it is common knowledge that even well-reviewed new books of poetry by established poets might sell merely a few hundred copies. I am grateful to Harry Chambers for telling me the following: SE sold over 3,000 copies; the Peterloo hardback of *Selected Poems* sold out (1,000) and WB, now reprinted, sold out its first (2,000) print run. VO and ST sold out in the paperback eds.

† U.A.Fanthorpe's father was a barrister.

behalf but this is the theme I recognise as having a call on me: people at the edges of things (as in, for instance, "Lament for the Patients" in *Standing To*). All the things you mention are also important of course.

EW: Do you actually *enjoy* writing poetry, or does it vary? Likewise, have you established for yourself writing habits that tend to be helpful to you (or have you idiosyncrasies you want to disclose, such as sleeping with moss under your pillow, like Yeats)? And does it all get harder or easier?

UAF: Well, sometimes it's great fun and it all comes flowing out; sometimes it's a penitential discipline over four years and more, and there are grudging little messages from time to time over the Muse's phone. What I like most of all is being in the middle of a poem that's going to achieve an end, to get somewhere. The worst moment of all is when you've finished a good one and haven't something to go on to next! I like waking in the middle of the night and thinking about something I'm in the middle of writing. No, I don't put moss under the pillow! When I was beginning to write poems, having a forty-minute lunchbreak (with no possibility of an extension) was very helpful to me. My main writing habit is carrying things about in my head and working on them as I walk or drive or in trains and so on. Washing-up is a very useful exercise, too.

EW: You've also established yourself as a very popular and effective reader of your poems in a variety of places, from pubs to the Albert Hall. To what extent does this side of your life as a poet influence what you write, do you think? And do you, in readings, read what you consider to be some of your best poems, or do you tend to read the ones which by now you know will probably go down well?

UAF: The fact that I read doesn't influence what I write at all — I write "what comes" (not "I'll sit down and write a poem for a reading"). I don't in my readings present poems that are hard to understand *for listeners* (as distinct from "readers"). I have some faithful standbys that I use. — I'm not sure that I *know* which my "best" poems are. When I read, it's partly a matter of mood or the nature of the audience or what the particular circumstances of the reading are or whether Rosie's there, and so on. I try to strike a balance between what I think they'll like and what I want to read.

EW: Are you aware of having been influenced by particular poets past and present? Browning and Chaucer seem obvious mentors from the past and Larkin and John Betjeman from our own times. How far do you consider you have a *distinctive* voice? (One for me again ...?)

UAF: Browning and Chaucer, yes — also Wordsworth as 'Idiot Man'!* Also Marvell. Present day poets ... not really Philip Larkin or John Betjeman — I learned a bit about verse form from Larkin but couldn't aspire to his "illuminations", nor would I try. John Betjeman I like but he isn't an influence. John Berryman, Geoffrey Hill, Akhmatova, Akhmedulina *are* important. As for any "distinctive voice", I'm interested in "voices", as in *ONLY HERE FOR THE BIER*, etc., and I enjoy working on voices for people in the Browning way. But they're of course modern voices. I try *not* to appear as a person myself.

EW: Following from that: how do you fit into the current poetry scene, do you think? I mean, in some ways you can be called a traditionalist (e.g. in texture, you take great pains to "get the words right", which many of our contemporaries do not; and in your "stance" you tend to respect roots, the abiding good things of the past). And do you feel reassured about the way things are or the way they're going (wherever *that* is ...) in poetry in this country? Do you have any thoughts about current publishing practices and tendencies or about the role of the Arts Council?

UAF: I never saw myself as part of any particular "school" — just as someone trying to find the words and patterns that would be best for a particular situation. I take *all* language as my province (including slang words, "rude" words, whatever) — use anything that's necessary to "get the words right".

Yes, the past *is* very important (not necessarily just because of "abiding good things", though — all of it is). I'm very encouraged by the way women are finding a voice in poetry — one of the better things about the current scene is that women are claiming a place. The larger "small" presses have kept going for so long — *that's* heartening too. Sad that the large chaps (I mean the publishers) are so London-based and mercenary and unadventurous. The Arts Council and its offshoots are what the patron once was: at its best, it works well, and I've benefited from this (in for instance the S. Martin's Fellowship), and there's the Royal Society of Authors, the Hawthornden Trust, and other such organisations. But more and more Arts Coucil money seems to be going to large enterprises such as opera and the RSC. Enterprises for writers often involve uprooting them: it would be nice if one could be a "writer in residence" *at home*!

EW: The Romantics, for instance, had a clear and elevated set of notions about the role of poets in society: what are *your* views on what poetry is doing and ought to be doing? Is it a marginal activity or still of abiding

---

* Cf. "Three Wordsworth Women, 3. THE LAST" (Wordsworth's wife, Mary): 'Still she lived on, since somebody had to,/To name the Work (i.e. *The Prelude*) and nurse it into print,/As he had known she would, dear Idiot Man ...' (*A Watching Brief*, p. 16). The phrase is still enigmatic.

importance? And if there are things that ought to be done to improve the status or role of poetry in our society, what do you consider they are, and who should be helping to bring them about (for instance, how important is education or how important *could* it be)?

UAF: Poetry's probably doing OK. It's a marginalised activity not attracting money or publicity, so it can stay honest and independent. It can't do more because it hasn't the status. It's *because* it's a marginal activity that it's of abiding importance: something so "unimportant" maintains its distance from the corrupting influences of, for example, money or journalism. 'All a poet can do is warn.'*

This isn't what you mean by "education", but the Arvon Foundation does a marvellous job for children in the closed courses, as well as for adults. What it does is make one think of Robert Graves and his idea of a college for poets where apprentices work with practising poets on the problems and possibilities of writing.

EW: I know this question couldn't be answered precisely without delving into archives and manuscripts (and I don't suggest for a moment that this should happen!) — but, as far as you recall, does the chronology of the volumes reflect the output of the poems?

UAF: Yes, it does. But one or two oddments may be of interest: e.g. "You will be hearing from us shortly" was submitted for *Side Effects* but Harry Chambers didn't like it: then he heard me read it and wanted it for *Standing To*†. I had writen "Patients" in time for *Standing To* and Harry wanted it for that, but I daren't let him have it as it was too obviously about the doctors etc. at the hospital where I worked‡.

EW: Is *Standing To*, a very long volume, something of an omnium gatherum, contemporary as far as the writing goes with *Side Effects*?

UAF: No, *Standing To* isn't contemporary with it: lots of different things had happened in the meantime — Mother died, and that gave me a great deal to write about: and in particular (as in "Rising Damp") her death made me realise what certain poems I'd been trying to write and hadn't been able to finish were actually about.

---

* Wilfred Owen's *Preface*.

† Where it now appears p. 44 and p. 64 (Peng)

‡ It appeared in *Voices Off* p. 21 and p. 94 (Peng)

EW: How do you enjoy the thought of being an 'A' Level set text? A back-handed compliment?

UAF: Quite irrelevant really. I wrote the poems out of my own needs and preoccupations. When they're published, they're little creatures walking off to lead their own lives. I'm glad if people find them useful. As for being an 'A' Level text, it depends very much on whether the teacher really wants to teach the poems — a good teacher can put over almost anything. What worries me is whether students will feel so alienated they'll hate me for ever. — It took *me* a long time to forgive Gray his "Elegy".

EW: Would it be true to say that you are more concerned to get the words right than to make patterns? There's a lot of blank verse in your poetry, and some formal things such as sonnets, and much organisation of poems into verse symmetry; but you prefer on the whole, don't you, a free but not outrageously-free verse that accomodates cadence and meaning rather than supplies Procrustean beds?

UAF: I'm *most* concerned with trying to find out and put down faithfully what it is that's trying to get itself said (which I really don't know, just have an inkling about). To begin with, I was interested in metrics and versification and still am up to a point if I feel it contributes — but there was a point, somewhere mid-*Standing To*, when I saw I'd get where I wanted to be by *breaking* the rules. I have a very important feeling that there's a right pattern for every poem — but "pattern" interpreted in its widest sense. If I'm lucky, that pattern will stamp itself on the first line and then I can just follow lead. I'm interested, too, in alliterative verse, e.g. in "Northmen"*. I like the thud of the iambic pentameter, but tend nowadays to use it rarely (because it's so strong). The trouble with verse symmetry is that it tends to use a lot of energy — I like to "run" the energy of a poem in a less obvious way, so the burden is carried by the imagery, or something which is actually unsaid. For example, "A Wartime Education"† — which is about hatred and not hatred. It doesn't actually *say* the wolf-whistling soldiers are on the way to fight for me. I don't want the reader to anticipate — rhyming verse is rather dangerous in this respect.

EW: Finally — I have to try asking — if the Muse continues to be kind, would you hope (or are you superstitious about that kind of hoping?) that your poetry would continue to follow its nose and your developing interests, or have you secret plans for it? — Daft question, but readers are always wanting to know aren't they?

* *Voices Off*, p. 28

† *A Watching Brief*, p. 29

UAF: My plans involve extra-poetic activity, really: two novels and a radio play are in my head just now.

What I'd like to manage in poetry is a collection in which every element would relate to the title, but the way each related to the others would change the meaning of all of them. But the poetry *does* seem to follow its nose, and perhaps it's wise to think of it as responding to events, rather than my being in control of it.

September 1993

Appendix C: Extracts from reviews

The appearance of a first collection of verse of the quality of U.A. Fanthorpe's *Side Effects* is an event to be celebrated. To read only a handful of these 40-odd poems is to be at once aware of a new and original voice in English poetry: clear, distinctive, and remarkably assured. The author, born 1929, can hardly be said to have rushed into print. This, in turn, may suggest that the very obvious technical skills and subtle awareness of the possibilities of language displayed here are the result of a long and arduous apprenticeship; but whatever the reasons, *Side Effects* is something well-worth waiting for ... U.A. Fanthorpe is closely acquainted with the kingdom of the "officially" sick, in institutions and the like. With a mercilessly exact yet compassionate eye she explores the lives of the sad, the mad, the unloved; delineates, with marvellous insight, the "other" world — at once comic and tragic — that is at the same time the perfect mirror of our own ... When dealing with landscape, as opposed to primarily the human scene, Miss Fanthorpe's touch is rather less sure ... Adjectives, now and then, give Miss Fanthorpe a bit of trouble and make unwarranted break-ins ... But these are flecks in the sun. *Side Effects*, beautifully produced and a pleasure to handle, is the most accomplished first book of poems I have come across in several years.

Charles Causley (SE) *S.W.*, May/June 1979

' ... She places her considerable technical accomplishement at the service of two worlds: a world of people, actual and unique in their chosen or unchosen predicaments, and one of place and historical event brooding beyond and behind the horizons of her human subjects. Her personality is revealed not by disclosure, but by the quality of a look focused sharply on something quite other. She is The Watcher, patient for glimpses of life which remain elusive, secretive; she is concerned with 'The very old, the mad, the failures' ... The group of poems which follows shows a deep understanding of place, a deep affection for Englishness and a country

> Bright with resourcefulness and smelling
> Of rain. This narrow island charged with echoes
> And whispers snares me.

These poems are more strongly built, making elaborate spaces for the bricks and grass; we grow conscious of buried life. The houses and the landscapes founder into weed or preserve their varied rituals in ways unseen by their creators; the old die singly in rooms vacated by the Edwardian week-end guests, behind windows which front lawns where Oberon's court shimmers the imagination. Places preserve their identities precariously under passing weathers, tease us with their flotsam and jetsam, focus for us the passing shows of life and death which open and close the collection ... *Side Effects* is, to my mind, one of the most arresting first collections of the last few years: mature, adroit, rich in its textures.

Peter Scupham (SE), *PN Review* Vol 6/4, 1979

U.A. Fanthorpe's first collection is pleasantly offered in an agreeable format from Peterloo Poets ... . *Side Effects* is partly just that: the poems that have accrued in lunch hours and other snatched moments during Miss Fanthorpe's working day as a hospital clerk. Poetry about occupations is now filling the gap left by the dying out of the last war service poetry of 1939-45. But what makes *Side Effects* a distinctly promising first book is a detached, observer's eye which can reshuffle experience of this life in a manner which is at once compassionate and disconcerting; and there is already a considerable technical maturity. If the case-history poems, though beautifully done, are somehow *expected*, Miss Fanthorpe's slant on the yachting "Specialist" with the fog-horn voice is not:

> *His heart is in*
> *His dinghy, where he can be cock*
> *Of the whole thwart, no space there for*
> *Subordinates.*
>
> *I am ashamed*
> *To be annoyed by his brutal*
> *Rejection of delicacy*
> *When he*
>
> *Pours out so much*
> *Of his ichor, modulates so*
> *Touchingly his loud-hailer, for*
> *His land-sick patients.*

"After Visiting Hours" adds its own extra dimension to the world of that most famous and moving of all modern hospital poems, Philip Larkin's "The Building"; I haven't seen this idea treated elsewhere. And there is a nice line in baroque fantasy, or allegory, in "My Brother's House" and "Family Entertainment". This is a varied, as well as a skilful and accomplished talent, and I look forward to more of these scathing or tender poems; "earthed", as she has it, in a poem with that title, in an English landscape which she invests with a very individual freshness and oddity, full of

... supermarkets

Where the cashiers' rudeness is native
To the district, though the bread's not, or gardens
Loved more than children,

Bright with resourcefulness and smelling
Of rain.

Alan Brownjohn (SE), *Encounter*

... These poems have a military air, not only on account of the title poems and the apposite cover drawing, but because of the prevailing sense of watchfulness, a guarded vigilance of observation and response. They report on experience with exactitude and a resourceful tactical deployment of linguistic tools.

Their language is sinewy, direct, not burdened with confusing similes. The poems work through descriptive notation rather than through metaphor or parable or literary allusion; and their mythological references are specific. "At the Ferry" portrays hospital patients as waiting on the banks of Charon's river, and this without any sense of contrivance or mental trickery. The mythology is rediscovered; one could say of this poem as the poem itself says of a woman patient, that 'her mind deferred to another dimension'. That 'deferred' is characteristic in its (very faint) tinge of irony, its ghost of a smile ...

Her touch is less sure with the extended conceit or metaphor: something prosaic, over-schematic about her imagination takes over. In "The Conductor" for instance, you read the poem in order to see how the author is going to work out her idea: I get the feeling that this may well be an early poem ...

U.A. Fanthorpe is sensitive to contrasting worlds. "Half Term" exemplifies the gift perfectly, making the tension between school life and home life bear quite a different significance from that normally attributed to it. Rules are easier to live with than love is: of such is the kingdom of this world.

Glen Cavaliero (ST), *The Present Tense* 4, 1983

... Her poems are particularly good when they offer unaffected voices from a gallery of human types that do not usually figure in poetry: patients in mental hospitals, army wives, people who practise hang-gliding. They speak an often humorous, often painful stoic wisdom. The book presents us with eight sections, the first of which, *STATIONS*

UNDERGROUND, deals with the underworld and its denizens. These poems juxtapose past and present, the mythical and the quotidian. In "At the Ferry" different scales of suffering take on the even grey of the Styx. A patient in hospital studies her magazine:

> *Is a registry office marriage*
> *Second-best? I suffer from a worrying*
> *Discharge from my vagina.*

The problem dissolves to a brief, haunting glimpse of the poet in her youth who sees Charon in the form of a boatman leaning by his punt-pole on an Oxford river. We rarely get such glimpses, though, for she prefers to deflect attention away from herself on to some other person — Tennyson, for example, whose death leads her to a moving contemplation of our ways of dying. Like a good teacher (she was indeed a teacher for many years) Fanthorpe gives us lessons in a dramatic fashion without embarrassing us. "Prolepsis", in the second section, teaches us how to act out old age; it is a chilling lesson.

Georgre Szirtes (ST), *Times Literary Supplement*, July 15th 1983

... When she turns to writing of places, her allusions come more from folklore than from literature, but her landscape is always peopled and its mythological content is always presented as a secondary feature to its tangible, geographic reality. So the rivers of '*Phlegethon, Acheron, Lethe, Styx*' are recalled in order to give a new dimension to the underground streams of London, '*Wandle, Walbrook, Tyburn, Fleet*'; and the Authurian legends associated with the hill fort of South Cadbury and Glastonbury's Isle of Avalon, separated by 'twelve miles of commonplace Somerset' bring dreams of knights into a teasing juxtaposition beside 'The native cattle, with their slow/Honourable look'.

Nearly all U.A. Fanthorpe's verse has this startling quality of admitting the commonplace, by accepting and transforming it into a prism which reflects the many facets of human concern, sympathy and wit. She never relinquishes the writer's first task, which is to hold the reader's attention; and she never does that by taking short cuts and betraying the authentic in literature and life. Nor is she one to repeat herself; and I would guess that her main line of development will be towards a more cryptic and enigmatic verse. ...

Shirley Toulson (ST), *South West Review* 15, November 1982

... Ursula Fanthorpe's new collection hovers on the edge of gentility but the body-count is high enough to make the final effect more astringent. The title sugggests her mission to let ordinary people have their say, sharply felt characters crowding the pages, bit-players from Robert Armin to Arthur Lowe, their brief moment centre stage recorded with a calm stoical precision. Even in her minatures there is the sense of a larger perspective, as in "Grandfather's Footsteps" where the old man feeding the birds on the lawn is a pawn in a deadlier game:

> Something is watching him,
> Silent and patient, coaxing him along
> With little crying fits and wheezy spells ...

... Though exits engage her more often than entrances the section *MILES TO GO* turns an affectionate eye on the young, especially those baffled by Eng. Lit. or "Being a Student" in general:

> My spelling mistakes are old
> Friends to my new tutor. He keeps
> Calling me Mandy, too ...

Yet there is no hint of superiority or envy; she is witty without being catty and there is a warmth often missing in Larkin, the poet she most closely resembles. Not all the poems feel the obligation to be deeply serious, but there is an openness to experience of all kinds which makes them always stimulating.

John Saunders (VO), *Stand Magazine* Vol. 28/2, Spring 1987.

Her best poems are those in which she manages to catch us by surprise, in spotting the pathos of the commonplace where we had not previously looked for it; in the visitors' book of a church, in laughing women, in a seminar on the verse of Robert Frost.

George Szirtes (VO), *Critical Quarterly*, Vol. 27, no. 2

The title of her book is apt. Some of these poems are not only the fruit of observation but also about the value of observation — observation so accurate that it becomes an intellectual and emotional exercise, not least in the setting-down. The cover illustration (always a feature of Peterloo Poets) is Filde's "The Doctor" (in the Tate), and in Fanthorpe's poem about it she says: 'The Doctor,/Who has done all he can, and knows nothing/Will help or heal, sits raptly, raptly,/As if such absorbed attention were in itself/A virtue. As it is.'. Poem after poem entertains and enlightens, and really there is little slackening throughout the book ... she knows very well what she is about: it is extremely reassuring to find her returning in the last section of the book to poems of full power (one about Sutton Hoo especially excellent). In this section, too, is a poem ("Garden Planning") that conveniently illustrates her talent for observation — 'Buttercups throttle with/Claw feet ... /More civilised mint advances neatly,/Pawn by indigo pawn.'

Roy Fuller (WB), *The Spectator*, January 30th 1988.

... All of the forty-odd poems seem to me complete successes, with the possible exception of "Washing-Up", in which domestic memories seem a little too cosily romanticized, and the doubtfully judged "Authorised Version", where the poet adopts a 20th-Century, and rather butch, vernacular for her dramatized gloss on the gospel story of Martha complaining to Jesus about Mary's failure to help with the chores. Elsewhere Fanthorpe shows a quite remarkably sharp ear for the forms and cadences of idiomatic speech: "Dear Mr Lee", which was commissioned by the Cheltenham Festival for a programme celebrating the life and work of Laurie Lee, captures perfectly the voice and attitudes of a bright, slightly rebellious teenage schoolgirl in a funny and touching tribute which must have delighted the author of *Cider with Rosie*, and in "Travelling Man" she displays a fine ear for the rhythms, vocabulary and syntax of working-class Lancashire. In the first person voice of "Downstairs at the Orangerie" the stiffer, more formal vernacular of a petty official is employed and, like Browning in his dramatic monologues, she communicates to the reader far more than the idiosyncracies of the individual through whom she speaks.

Vernon Scannell (WB), *The Poetry Review* Vol. 77/4, Winter 1987/8.

U.A. Fanthorpe is adept at the kind of poem most poets would balk at: her commissioned poem for Laurie Lee, "Dear Mr Lee", takes enormous risks in being written as an innocent paean from an adolescent girl, but she carries it off triumphantly. She has a sure sense of ironic juxtaposition, as the girl's love of *Cider with Rosie* contends with examination questions ('*social welfare in the rural community* / and *the seasons as perceived by an adolescent*'), the teacher's scorn for Spanish fantasies ('all Timeshare villas/and Torremolinos'). This poem encapsulates U.A. Fanthorpe's defence of the ordinary human response against academicism and the encroachments of our late-20-century media-mangled sensibility. She votes for decency and comes up 'bright and strange' with every book.

Peter Forbes (WB), *The Listener*, 25th February 1987.

... There is a deceptiveness in this poetry: it speaks in the voice of our daily life in its mundanity and occasional glory, its pathos and humour, toughness and tenderness, strength and weakness. It celebrates an amazing variety of characters and includes four-footed companions and other creatures that share our world, and describes their quirks of character without falling into the trap of anthropomorphism.

Fanthorpe's use of language is so masterly that it becomes unobtrusive with its tight economy, hardly any rhyme, its quiet music and unerring choice of words. In the new collection there is a pleasing amount of well-controlled alliteration. In "Superannuated Psychiatrist" for instance:

> Old scallyway scapegoat has skedaddled,
> Retired at last to bridge and both kinds of bird-watching.

These two lines serve as an example for typical Fanthorpe devices — the alliteration, which occurs on the first line, three 'sk' words each perfect for its purpose, a gentle dig at a profession which can sometimes produce slightly wicked practitioners; the long-suffering scapegoat for our confessed guilts and problems; and the nice feel of one scampering and scurrying off with relief; followed by the delicious bevy of 'b' words. A fine instance indeed of poetic compression! ... Characterisation is a strong aspect of Fanthorpe's work, observation and heard voice used to produce a convincing and clear portrait lit by understanding and compassion in the manner of Rembrandt, a portrait that speaks plainly, whose spirit shines through the words. Surely no poet writing now can match her for clarity and charity; and for, in every sense, pure poetry ...

Anne Born (N-V), *Envoi 103*, Autumn 1992.

... Though her sympathies for the suffering are never in doubt, her poems aren't maudlin. There is, rather, a bracing, no-nonsense quality to much of the work that makes possible moments of tenderness all the more affecting for their unexpectedness. It's a quality very much in evidence in "Dear Sir", a brisk elegy for a Scottish doctor, in which Fanthorpe good-humouredly accuses her subject of, among other things, worrying about patients after hours, of concealing his wartime bravery, 'Of inconspicuous valour on behalf of underdogs' and 'of mixing the genres,/Of playing Quixote in Sancho Panza's clothes.' To 'accuse' her subject of his quiet good-deeds is masterly, a fine balance between praise and playfulness. There is a playfulness, too, in the clerk respectfully addressing her late superior 'Sir'; this also floats the idea of chivalry, picked up in the reference to Cervantes' knight and squire. The poem builds, on these devices, to an almost unbearably moving climax:

> O Sir, I accuse you of dying at home,
> In bed, asleep, without a hint of impaired
> Cortical integrity;

That poetic 'O Sir' is perfectly balanced by the prosaic, cruelly matter-of-fact 'impaired/Cortical integrity' ...

Stephen Knight (N-V), *London Magazine*, August/September 1993

U.A. Fanthorpe is, among other and bleaker things, a bit of a tease. The ordinarily ill-informed reader will have to wait until page 58 of her new collection for a footnote elucidating the book' title: here he will learn that the source is the first verse of Psalm 51 (which, though Ursula Fanthorpe doesn't say so, is 'Have mercy upon me, O God, according to thy loving kindness: according to the multitude of thy tender mercies blot out my transgressions'), and that until 1827 was the trial verse for anyone claiming Benefit of Clergy. If you could read it, you saved your neck.

The note is prompted by a poem actually called "Word Games", of which there are plenty in the book: a fable about different kinds of childish time ('Gettinguptime, timeyouwereofftime' and so on); a watch playing the *'doo dah doo dah dey'* of "Camptown Races"; a rat-a-tat drumming toy's complaint; a cat 'purring in German'. The opening poem, a lightweight and unfunny piece called "As Well as the Bible and Shakespeare ...?", seems an odd choice until you realize that the poems are arranged, with arbitrary word-gaminess, in alphabetical order of titles, which seems odder still.

... her writing's distinctive character springs form a head-on collision between a scholarly, riddling, crossword-solving disposition (the first part of "Word Games" comes complete with clues and solutions) and the world she has chosen to inhabit since she left teaching in 1970. Her work as a hospital clerk has given her, like her near-contemporary Elizabeth Bartlett, both a sceptical view of humanity and a specific anecdotal theme which she has explored in earlier poems such as "Lament for the Patients" and two called "Casehistory". Here she returns, in "Back to the Front", to a context in which people are still objects, neutralized by 'Prim Clinical diction', but objects have become threats:

> Instead there are new toys, compact, intense
> User-unfriendly. The photocopier will mug me
> If I face it alone. The phone is tapped
> By a sharp inquisitor, who calculates my fear.
> This wallpaper, with its lilt of country kitchens,
> Was chosen to deceive. ...

Things are not quite as they seem outside the hospital, either.

Among Fanthorpe's characteristic modes is a sort of impacted personal anecdote, its data as obliquely and tantalizingly disarranged as a case for Inspector Morse: one poem, "Escaping", addressed to an unspecified 'You', seems to be about an elderly relative's odd reading habits, and only in the last two lines discloses itself as an elegy for her father; another, "Neighbours", deploys its foreground subject of doves and blackbirds essentially to counterpoint the uncomprehending reticence of the humans beyond the fence.

Human and even superhuman communication is fraught with misunderstanding: poor Titania, bored with immortality, scornful of her supposed 'hallucination', confesses her abiding love for Bottom's 'understated donkey dignity', his perishably mortal life of 'The last pint, high blood pressure, accident, prose'. Fanthorpe, too, casts her vote for that prose integrity, which is why her wry moments of celebration carry absolute conviction, as in "May 8th: how to recognise it": here tulips have been beheaded after 'their showy conversation' and wallflowers 'have turned bony', but limes have the look of someone long-silent who "'is about to say a very good thing' and roses 'hang about humbly in the wings'. Hers is a world grown triumphantly beyond the easy delusions of spring.

Neil Powell (N-V), *Times Literary Supplement*, November 20th, 1992

There is something marginal about U.A. Fanthorpe. And it is about not standing in the centre of art or life shouting "Poet, Carer, Transcendentalist!" It is more about naming your volumes *Side Effects*, *Standing To*, and *Voices Off*; about describing yourself as 'the artist, the typist' or 'Not a nice person'; above all, about having a voice which speaks cooly, wryly, often 'Masking by instinct', playing with the 'arcane litany of cliché'.

For U.A. Fanthorpe to stand on the margin of life, putting herself deprecatingly in the category of "wallflower" or ruefully acknowledging distance in family relationships, or in a hospital job, is what enables her 'to be a connoisseur' of other people's lives, fictional or actual and to interrogate compulsively and compellingly the other life beyond death.

If this be "marginality", let's have more of it ... Her favoured short lines and stanzas communicate the impression of a mind at play to humorous or serious purpose, the two often being indivisible. Her style and her philosophy aptly fit a poet who can wittily sum up Patience Strong as 'feathering her inglenook' and then chooses as the closing line of her poem the epileptic patient's words of praise for 'Some cosy musing in the usual vein,/And *See*, he said, *this is what keeps me going*.' U.A. Fanthorpe has once again made herself marginal, wittily, sensitively, and exactly the right thing to do to produce her fine and particular poetry.

Pam Barnard (Peng), *Poetry Wales*, *23/1*, November 1987.

... There is no question in my mind that U.A. Fanthorpe would like to be read by the sort of people she writes about: the patients, clerks and nurses, the first-year students, the frowsty women dons, the balding gardener, the irascible heroic friend reading Cowper while he battles cancer ...
They (Mitchell and Fanthorpe) are modest in the manner of Pym or Powys, a self-imposed modesty we Americans more often associate with novelists, who are entitled to pick a locale, a particular subgroup of the human species for their observations, inventions and obsessions. These two poets are modest in the manner of Philip Larkin ... and if neither of them exercises his technical bravura, they have, both, a largesse of spirit, manifested by intellectual curiosity and a compassion untinged with condescension that was largely foreign to him ... Fanthorpe and Mitchell are looking more outward than inward, and their self-reflection, when it is there, although it can be blunt, and looks into the abyss more than once, refuses despair ...

Marilyn Hacker "Unauthorised Voices: the work of U.A. Fanthorpe and Elma Mitchell", *Grand Street* (USA), Autumn 1989.

This *Selected Poems* is drawn from three collections originally published between 1978 and 1984 by Peterloo Poets. The poems present us with a rich array of different voices and characters, often taking the form of monologues. In one poem, "Growing Up", U.A. Fanthorpe defines her role:

> Called to be a connoisseur, I collect
> Admire, the effortless bravura
> Of other people's lives, proper and comely ...

Though in many ways she is a self-effacing poet, more concerned with 'other people's lives', this seems too detached as a description of what she is doing and the kind of compassion and attention she shows. For the characters she seems most interested in are non-central, the marginal, the overlooked, those whose voices are not heard within the literary tradition, 'the voices off', as she calls one of her collections. Many of her earlier poems arise out of her experience of working in a hospital, and in a world of "The List", the name of one poem, she lets vulnerable human voices speak to us. In poems like the two "Casehistory ... " poems a damaged articulacy also says something about the limits of articulacy, the bleak experience of suffering that cannot be transcended. In other poems like the wonderfully witty "For Saint Peter" there is also a kind of joy in the uncontainable, disruptive nature of people's lives.

My favourite poems are those which situate us at the edge of literature allowing "difference" to open up perspectives, questioning formality with colloquial informality. In the four interlinked poems ONLY HERE FOR THE BIER the masculine world of Shakespearian tragedy is seen from a "woman's angle". This is Gertrude in *Hamlet* as mother-in-law:

> Such a nice girl. Just what I wanted
> For the boy. Not top drawer, you know,
> But so often, in our posisition, that
> Turns out to be a mistake ...

Other poems bring different points of view together: in "Knowing the Sonnet" it is critic and poem, in "Seminar: Felicity and Mr Frost" it is child and poem; there is always a sense of discovering alternative meanings, experience beyond the formal artefact. The last poem in the volume, "From the Third Story", juxtaposes the traditional restraint of the woman writer's life with the 'mad' voice of repressed power. It is fitting that this volume, itself always moving between power and restraint, shoul end by setting this voice free:

> *Now at last I know*
> *Why I was brought here*
> *And what I have to do.*

Linda Anderson (Peng), *Writing Women*, Vol 4 No. 2

The cover of U.A. Fanthorpe's *Selected Poems* shows a detail from "The Weighing of the Heart of the Scribe Ani" (Egyptian, British Museum), and this is fitting because Ms. Fanthorpe is known as one of the principal Muses of the N.H.S., and her hospital poems might well be considered as the Weighing of the Heart of the Clerk Fanthorpe. Though her compassionate heart is by no means found wanting, perhaps a reviewer should concentrate on weighing her wit, as there is much more to her work than the Poetry in the Pity (as there is on Owen also).

Clerk Fanthorpe is deeply versed in Classical Mythology, as is shown in "Sisyphus", "Janus", and "Pomona Vertumnus", and she has roots in the English landscape, as in "Earthed", "Stanton Drew", "Canal: 1977" and the marvellous "Palimpsest", and she acknowledges a family, as in "My Brother's House", "Fanfare" (for her mother), and "Father in the Railway Buffet". But education, roots and relatives are commonplace among poets; real talent and serious wit are less so. The wit is a principal means to the person of the Roman God of the New Year and other Thresholds.

Without formal rhyming, this poem is nevertheless musical, ringing the changes through words that are almost anagrams, one of another.

>   ... My emblems are albums,
> The bride's mother's orchid corsage, the dark cortège

It starts lightly — 'Lord of the Lupercal and the Letts diary' — but becomes more sad and serious, although a hot-bed of puns:

> Master of the silent passacaglia
> Of the future, I observe the dancers
> But never teach them the step.
>
> I am the birthday prescience
> Who knows the obituary ...

Janus marks time;

> I am the future's overseer, the past's master.
> See all, know all, speak not.
> I am the two-faced god.

Anna Adams (Peng) *Acumen 4*, October 1986

    U.A Fanthorpe has a great gift for pictorially precise similes. One poem ("After Visiting Hours") tells how 'Darkness descends like an eyelid', while another ("Fanfare") remembers her father with ' ... his swimmimg togs/Tucked like a swiss roll under his arm'. ... Many of her poems deal with the distress associated with hospitals. She documents case histories, portrays suffering patients, observes hospital visitors crying like gulls. Like Philip Larkin she is able to transform apparently ordinary scenes into richly resonant scenarios.

    On the evidence of this book, U.A. Fanthorpe is a poet of real importance. She is shrewd, intelligent, imaginatively alert, technically adroit and emotionally appealing: a writer who can both edify and entertain.

Alan Bold (Peng), *The Scotsman*, 5th July 1986

Appendix D: Select Bibliography

Features, articles, biographies and interviews:

Connie Bensley and Judith Kazantzis: "Dropping Out and Standing To" — interview with UAF, *PEN 20*, Spring 1986.

Sara Davies: interview with UAF, *Arts West*, September 1988.

U.A. Fanthorpe: "Slow Learner", *Poetry Matters No. 5*, (ed. Harry Chambers) Peterloo Poets, Winter 1987.

U.A. Fanthorpe: "Scenes from a Provincial Life", *Country Living 51*, March 1990.

Diana Hendry: interview with UAF, *Gloucestershire & Avon Life*, August 1985.

Derek Weeks: "Fanthorpe's Rhyme and Reason", *Gloucestershire & Avon Life*, April 1987.

See also **Appendix C** for selected reviews.

SAFE AS HOUSES

by U.A. Fanthorpe

publication October 1995

Safe as Houses is best-selling poet U.A. Fanthorpe's 6th individual volume to be published by Peterloo. The "safe" houses in this volume include both real and fictional houses, for example, houses damaged in the Blitz, Ibsen's *A Doll's House*, and the Macbeths' castle, Dunsinane. Houses become a metaphor for the world, and U.A. Fanthorpe writes of all the loving, cruel, and stupid things we do in our world 'house'. As in her previous volumes, U.A. Fanthorpe writes poems that are moving, disturbing and funny. The volume includes Christmas poems, poems concerned with painting, craft and magic, and poems that are revisions of the classics, notably one adding an extra scene to *Macbeth*.

From a review of *Selected Poems:*

> 'For U.A. Fanthorpe to stand on the margin of life, putting herself deprecatingly in the category of "wallflower" or ruefully acknowledging distance in family relationships, or in a hospital job, is what enables her "to be a connoisseur" of other people's lives, fictional or actual and to interrogate compulsively and compellingly the other life beyond death.
> If this be 'marginality', let's have more of it ... Her favoured short lines and stanzas communicate the impression of a mind at play to humorous or serious purpose, the two often being indivisible ... U.A. Fanthorpe has once again made herself marginal, wittily, sensitively — and exactly the right thing to do to produce her fine and particular poetry.'
> — **Pam Barnard** *Poetry Wales*, **23/1**, November 1987.

72 pages, laminated paperback.   ISBN 1 871471 59 1

£6.95 post free from **PETERLOO POETS,
2 KELLY GARDENS, CALSTOCK, CORNWALL PL18 9SA, U.K.**